Black Women's Experiences of Criminal Justice

A Discourse on Disadvantage

Ruth Chigwada-Bailey

Foreword by Sylvia Denman CBE

WATERSIDE PRESS
WINCHESTER

Black Women's Experiences of Criminal Justice
A Discourse on Disadvantage

Published 1997 by
WATERSIDE PRESS
Domum Road
Winchester SO23 9NN
Telephone or Fax 01962 855567
INTERNET:106025.1020@compuserve.com

ISBN Paperback 1 872 870 54 6

Cataloguing-in-Publication Data A catalogue record for this book can be obtained from the British Library

Cover design John Good Holbrook Ltd, Coventry

Printing and binding Antony Rowe Ltd, Chippenham.

Black Women's Experiences of Criminal Justice

CONTENTS

Foreword *vii*

Acknowledgements *x*

CHAPTER

1 A Combination of Forces *11*
2 Voices Unheard *21*
3 Police and Black Women *29*
4 Probation and Black Women *49*
5 Experience of the Courts *63*
6 Beatrice's Case *87*
7 Black Women and Imprisonment *101*
8 Hopes and Ambitions *121*

Appendix I : Historical Background to Modern-Day Problems of 'Immigrant' Labour in Britain *135*

Index *137*

Foreword

There has been, in recent years, an encouraging increase in the attention given to issues of race as they affect the position of ethnic minorities within the criminal justice system. This focus was given impetus by section 95 Criminal Justice Act 1991 which for the first time by statute imposed a duty on those involved in the administration of justice to avoid discrimination on the grounds of race or gender—or, indeed, on any other improper ground. A number of influential studies, some of them mentioned in this book, act as a reminder of the need for this provision which requires the Home Secretary to publish relevant information annually. These and other data have done much to raise awareness of the way in which minority ethnic groups, in particular Afro-Caribbean people, have been disadvantaged in matters of criminal justice. There is now a growing body of evidence documenting the extent to which discrimination occurs at various stages in the process including in court proceedings, prisons, and in the work of the police and of probation services. Culture, class and a complicated nexus of factors contribute to explaining the reasons underlying unequal handling but it is now clear that skin colour provides a vital key to understanding these patterns. These factors seem to have impacted disproportionately on black people and on women and this contributes to understanding black over-representation in the prison population.

In this book, Ruth Chigwada-Bailey seeks to extend our knowledge in a fresh direction by directly retelling personal experiences which inform us about the perspectives of black women who have actually been through the criminal justice process. They have found themselves on the wrong side of the law, ultimately in prison, and have experienced at first hand the sense of powerlessness which results from their strong feeling that something is not quite right about the way they have been treated. A recent study by NACRO graphically presents the particular problems which generally beset women prisoners, a small but worryingly increasing section of the prison population. They bring into prison with them intense problems of family, home, caring and community, and the response from a system geared to handling men has been less than adequate in meeting their needs.

What these women say, albeit from what some people might feel is the biased standpoint of those who have been convicted and imprisoned, deserves to be listened to. It is some of the best information we have about the lives of such women, who, according to the statistics, are not only currently appearing in record numbers in our prisons, but appear to be suffering proportionately higher penalties for their offences. Black women face multiple hazards of discrimination through race, gender and social class. The much trumpeted efforts in the last decade or so to address problems of black disadvantage in criminal justice agencies have not yet delivered anything like the even-handed justice which is the declared aim of equality policies. Ruth Chigwada-Bailey, in setting out these experiences drawn directly from the testimony of black women trapped in the system, subtitles her work, 'A Discourse on Disadvantage'. We should listen to the women in the book and I hope it will reach many people concerned with the administration of criminal justice. They are bound to be affected by the immediacy of the problems made real through the eloquent account of how a criminal justice system, full of good intentions, is failing to respond in a way which capitalises on awareness of these experiences.

Sylvia Denman CBE
Former Member of the Criminal Justice Consultative Council
April 1997

For my late parents

Rina and John Chigwada

Acknowledgements

The work from which this book derives would not have been possible without the participation of the women interviewed. To them all I am more than grateful for volunteering to share their experiences with me.

I am also very grateful to Jill Radford for looking at my first draft and for her constructive criticisms, and indebted to Angela Devlin for her invaluable help and encouragement.

Special thanks go to my husband Philip whose help, love and sense of humour kept me going when writing the book.

Ruth Chigwada-Bailey

April 1997

Chapter 1

A Combination of Forces

This book considers the way that disadvantage may become aggravated in the case of African-Caribbean women who find themselves on the wrong side of the criminal law. When this happens, the various stages which go to make up the criminal justice process of England and Wales[1] may be propelled by several forces—each constituting a hazard in itself—but which, *in combination*, create a greater potential for unequal treatment. These forces are:

- those which affect black[2] people, whatever their gender, living in a society where the dominant values, culture, institutions and sense of history are those of white people;
- those which affect women, whatever the colour of their skin, living in a society devised, organised and run primarily by men; and
- those which affect people, whatever their gender or the colour of their skin, at the lower end of the economic or social scale. It can be noted that a person's status in this regard may be partly influenced by either of the first two considerations.

For convenience, the three items will be referred to throughout this book as 'race', 'gender' and 'class'. It is not simply a question of adding together these various aspects of disadvantage, rather of considering the way in which they compound one another—my argument being that the whole is greater than the sum of the parts. The full situation is not readily discerned from existing research, which tends in the main (and maybe for practical reasons) to focus on one aspect of disadvantage only. That is why this book is about *Black Women's Experiences of Criminal Justice*. It asks the reader to listen to what black women offenders have to say about matters. As Lord Elton, a former conservative Home Office minister, said during a House of Lords debate during the Criminal Justice Act 1991:[3]

---

[1] For an overview see *Introduction to the Criminal Justice Process*, Gibson B and Cavadino P, Waterside Press, 1995.

[2] The term 'black' is used in this work to refer to people of *African* descent. Except where the context clearly implies otherwise, the term 'ethnic minority' is reserved for other *non-white* groups such as people of Asian descent.

[3] For a note about section 95 see page 15.

I was a reluctant convert to the view that there appears to be an element of discrimination against ethnic minority offenders in our criminal processes . . . If a particular discrete, identifiable and self-identifiable sector of that society believes that there is a system of justice which is just for other people but not for them, whether or not that belief is well founded, the effects upon our society as a whole will be very damaging because they will see the judicial system not as a means of maintaining law and order but of keeping 'them' down and 'us' up.

Black women are one such 'discrete' and 'identifiable' sector. Whether their concerns are valid can only be assessed by drawing on what is known about discrimination against black people in general and against women—and then drawing the logical conclusion that it must be worse for people who fall into both categories. If what black women offenders *say* is consistent with known data then this is one further reason to listen to them, beyond that given by Lord Elton.

Race

There is no want of information to show that black people and certain other ethnic minorities feature disproportionately in the criminal justice process. If the prison population is taken as a main indicator of this, the mid-1995 *Prison Statistics* show that 18 per cent of all prisoners are from minority ethnic groups (17 per cent of male prisoners and 24 per cent of female prisoners) compared to 5.5 of the general population. Twelve per cent of the total prison population (11 per cent of males and 20 per cent of females) is classified as 'black' (as per the same classification as used in this book[4]). This compares with around 1.5 per cent of the general population.

Gender

On 7 March 1997 there were 2,476 women in prison out of a total prison population in England and Wales of 59,156, 4.2 per cent of the total compared with 3.1 per cent in 1985.[5] According to a paper published by the Penal Affairs Consortium:

Since the end of 1992, the courts have responded to the growing mood of toughness in penal policy by adopting a more punitive stance towards

---

[4] See footnote 2.

[5] 'Women, Sentencing and Prisons', Rutherford A, *New Law Journal*, 1997, 147, pp. 424–425.

women offenders. The number of women prisoners has risen almost twice as fast as the male prison population.[6]

Quite apart from the disproportionate increase in the number of women in prison there are further question marks concerning the nature of the offences for which they are imprisoned, the extent to which they are viewed as appropriate for certain types of sentence and the way in which they may be accelerated up the sentencing tariff. These issues are explored in later chapters.

Race and gender

Black women are a marginalised group. They are poorly represented in education, the professions, commerce, industry and politics. They suffer higher levels of unemployment than most other groups.

Critically, so far as the purposes of this book are concerned, their presence in the criminal justice process and in prison is disproportionate to their numbers in society in general. Thus, for example, at the time of writing, the most up to date published breakdown of the total female prison population by ethnic origin shows that of 1,804 women in prison on 30 June 1994:

- 1,355 (75 per cent) were white
- 370 (21 per cent) were black
- 27 (1 per cent) were South Asian
- 52 (3 per cent) were classified as 'Chinese or other'
- the relevant information for two women went unrecorded.[7]

In all, 25 per cent of female prisoners were from minority ethnic groups. Twelve per cent were British nationals and 13 per cent foreign nationals. By comparison, only 16 per cent of the male prison population on the same date were from minority ethnic groups.

Interest in black women among researchers has concerned mostly general aspects of their family life, employment and education. This preoccupation may be rooted in the notion of the 'enslaved black matriarch' who learnt to bring up her children in the absence of a husband and who is thus deserving of study because her behaviour is different from that of 'normal' women. As is argued in later chapters, it may well be because the stereotype of the black woman is of someone qualitatively different to her white counterpart that black

---

[6] 'The Imprisonment of Women: Some Facts and Figures', Penal Affairs Consortium, 1996.

[7] *Prison Statistics England and Wales 1995.*

13

women have tended to receive different treatment from the criminal justice agencies and to be viewed as 'capable of committing crime'.

Just how misleading stereotypes are can be seen from my own earlier research into the education of African-Caribbean girls[8] which shows that modern-day black fathers play a significant part in the education of their children, are proud of their achievements and do their best to help and encourage them to obtain better qualifications. As some of the girls in that study said:

> My father encouraged me to go for 'A' levels. He equated education with success. He says that being black you won't get anything without education.

> My father has always been very ambitious for us. He wants us to work hard at college so that we can get a job.

Closely related to stereotyping, black women may also suffer from 'secondary punishment' or what I will call 'guilt by association'. By being the mothers or sisters of black youths (themselves stereotyped as 'criminal') they may find themselves in trouble with the police—who may, for example, come to their homes to arrest or search for their menfolk (see further in *Chapter 3*). It can be argued that secondary punishment affects all black families in terms of harassment and in some cases brutality by the police and it can lead to questionable treatment, poor procedures, false accusations or malicious prosecutions—as a number of high profile cases have shown in recent times.

Class

Black women experience high levels of poverty, it being a feature of women in prison that they suffer this particular disadvantage. However, not all poor people commit crimes or end up in prison. For example, Bangladeshis, the group with the highest unemployment rate, are under-represented in prison. It does seem to follow, however, that if a woman belongs to a group which is both black (and therefore at extra risk of imprisonment) and poor (thus fitting a description which accords with that of other women in prison) then there is a greater, rather than a lesser, chance that she will end up in prison through a combination of factors within which poverty is subsumed.

---

[8] 'Not Victims Not Superwomen: The Education of Afro-Caribbean Girls', Chigwada R, *Spare Rib*, No. 183, 1987.

Section 95 and other developments

No book of this kind would be complete without reference to section 95 Criminal Justice Act 1991 which requires the Home Secretary to publish annually information which will facilitate the performance by persons engaged in the administration of criminal justice of 'their duty to avoid discrimination against any persons on the ground of race or sex or any other improper ground'. This is the first explicit recognition in statute law of the existence of a duty to avoid discrimination. Among a number of indications of unequal treatment, the first Home Office booklet issued pursuant to this provision noted that:

> Afro-Caribbeans in particular are very heavily over represented in prison. In 1986 they made up 8 per cent of sentenced male prisoners and 12 per cent of sentenced female prisoners. By 1990 these figures had increased to 10 per cent for males and 24 per cent for females. This apparently dramatic rise for women may be accounted for by an increase in those convicted of drug smuggling, many of whom are foreign nationals.

The publication of official information has continued and increased since 1991 and has been accompanied by a range of initiatives by the different criminal justice agencies designed to ensure equality of treatment and that discrepancies in the way cases are dealt with are identified and acted upon. They range from moves within the Lord Chancellor's Department and by the Judicial Studies Board (responsible for the training of judges), the Bar, Law Society and Crown Prosecution Service (each of which has developed codes of practice or policies designed to eliminate discrimination) and the police and prison service. In 1994 the Criminal Justice Consultative Council produced a report 'Race and the Criminal Justice System' containing 50 practical recommendations for criminal justice agencies and government departments, and in 1995 the Justices' Clerks' Society published a paper 'Black People in Magistrates' Courts' designed to increase awareness of the way black people may be treated by courts unless proper training and working methods are in place. Also, the Home Office has funded a NACRO project which provides information and help to agencies in the implementation and delivery of non-discriminatory policies.[9]

Despite the fact that some information about the treatment of black women has emerged as a result of the above strategies and initiatives

---

[9] The implementation and impact of section 95 is summarised in *Introduction to the Criminal Justice Process*, Gibson B and Cavadino P, Waterside Press, 1995; and in 'Race and Criminal Justice', Penal Affairs Consortium, September 1996. Where appropriate, relevant information has been incorporated into later chapters of this book.

(as indicated by the quotation towards the start of this section) none of these otherwise welcome measures have so far focused on black women as such.

THE INTERVIEWS

The treatment of black women as discussed in this book is based on lengthy and searching interviews I carried out with black women living in Britain who had become involved with the criminal justice process, this generally ending up with a prison sentence. There were 20 women in all and I asked them about the treatment they had received and their *perceptions* of events, which—whatever the actualities—were realities to them. The important thing was to listen to them to see whether anything might be learnt from overlapping comments or the fact that a point of view coincided with or was supported by other information.

I thus wrote to various organizations, working with women inside prison and after release, including the probation service. The letter explained that I was interested in talking to black women who had been in prison. As a result, I was put in touch with a black female prisoner and from this first contact word spread around women's prisons that I wished to interview black women about their experiences of the criminal justice process. Several other women telephoned or wrote from prison saying that they would be interested in taking part. This created a 'snowball' sample, in effect self-selected and voluntary. This had the advantage that the participants were both willing to talk and interested in the project. In fact, all the women demonstrated enthusiasm. They wanted to know why I was interviewing them, what I would do with their comments and how I came to think of the idea.

All of them were informed that everything they said was confidential and that their names would be changed in any subsequent publication.

The women in the sample
The profile of the women in the sample is as follows:

- sixteen were black British, i.e. born in Britain
- four were born outside Britain but had been living in this country for at least five years
- all were of African-Caribbean background
- their ages ranged from 21 years to 38 years

16

- for sixteen of the women it was their first time in trouble with the law and thus their first time in prison (where applicable)
- the other four had been in trouble with the law from the age of 12 or 13
- their offences ranged from fraud, shoplifting, handling stolen goods and drugs offences to robbery
- sixteen were unemployed at the time of arrest, one worked in the post office, one as a child minder and for the tourist board, one was a qualified secretary and another had an import and export business
- three possessed GCSE 'O' levels; the rest had left school without any qualifications
- two were in private rented accommodation; the rest lived in council properties (usually flats)
- eighteen were still in prison; the remaining two were on probation (but had previously been to prison)
- those women who *were* in prison were serving sentences of between 18 months and eight years
- eighteen were single, one was married and one divorced
- all the women had children and five of them had their children with them in prison.

Interview method

I conducted the interviews informally using a few headings to stimulate discussion. I allowed the women 10 to 15 minutes after each interview to ask me questions (unrelated to the interview if they so wished). In fact they asked a great many questions giving a degree of insight which bolstered understanding of their attitudes and reactions to the criminal justice process, for example, some of them wanted guidance with further education and some to talk about problems concerning accommodation after release: see *Chapter 8*.

The range of issues explored

I interviewed them about their experiences with the police, customs officers, solicitors, prison officers, barristers, probation officers, magistrates and judges. I asked the women to think back to the time when they were arrested and what transpired between then and the present time (when they were in prison or on probation).

I was particularly interested in exploring the women's perceptions of the following issues:

17

- How were they, as black women, treated by people within the criminal justice process?
- Were they seen as potential suspects or deserving of a particular kind of treatment?
- When arrested, were they accorded fair treatment and, for example, access to a lawyer?
- Did they think that they had received their 'just deserts' or were they aggrieved at their punishment?
- How did the stereotype image of the black woman fit with the dominant white ideology of a 'good' woman—that is, did their lifestyle meet expectations about the way women should behave?
- What part did their culture and race play from arrest to sentence?
- Did their cultural background have any bearing on decisions, for example to bring charges, on the risk that they might re-offend, on the jury's decision as to guilt or innocence, or the judge's or magistrates' decision about sentence?
- Did 'chivalrous treatment' play any part in the way they were treated?

I pointed out that I was unlikely to be shocked or offended by anything the women said, and encouraged them to talk freely about their experiences.

It may not be generally understood that many black women in prison are worried about their families and friends finding out about this because so much stigma can attach in a black community to being an ex-prisoner. I had to convince one woman from Nigeria that I was not Nigerian before she would agree to be interviewed so worried was she that the news might carry back home. Whilst there is no way of knowing, I have no special reason to believe that any of the women tried to mislead me or did not tell the truth concerning their *perceptions* (it is accepted that this is not quite the same thing as saying that the 'facts' they related or, in some cases, the allegations they made, are true or valid).

I was concerned to explore whether any differences in treatment accorded to women of different races might be attributed to rules, policies or directives within organizations, or to institutional or individual racism? In the following chapters, these questions are addressed by looking at what the women said and at some of the other information which is available about black people, women, crime and the criminal justice process.

Structure of the book

The following chapter looks at the need to hear the voice of black women when considering the causes of crime and when dispensing of criminal justice—and at the absence of black women's voice and experience in this debate. Feminist criminology has largely left out of account black women's specific experiences. Indeed, such studies have tended to focus on white women (and more general works on black men). The erroneous premise that such studies can be used to properly inform discussions about black women is challenged.

Chapter 3 examines the policing of black women and *Chapter 4* their involvement with the probation service. *Chapter 5* concentrates on the courts and sentencing. *Chapter 7* is about black women's experiences of prison.

Beatrice's Case

One woman who was unhappy with the way she had been treated by customs officers, the police and the courts asked me to attend the second hearing of her case. I also attended the third trial, as on the second hearing the jury could not reach a verdict. *Beatrice's Case* is described in some detail in *Chapter 6* if only to illustrate how the criminal justice process can be perceived by black women and possibly how it can go astray. It deals with white perceptions of black women's 'inferior' culture, looking at how race, gender and class are articulated from arrest to sentence.

Beatrice's case also sheds some light on how black professionals can be treated. Black lawyers can be at a disadvantage in court, and black people may even find themselves compelled to prefer representation by white lawyers. For convenience, this aspect is incorporated into the relevant part of *Chapter 5*, which deals with black women's experiences of courts and lawyers.

Looking ahead

The closing chapter deals with a number of points made by the women interviewed which I have drawn together under the title *Hopes and Ambitions*. I have added some points of my own concerning items raised throughout the text which people concerned with criminal justice might consider in order to better understand the position of black women.

Chapter 2

Voices Unheard

A black woman's experience of the criminal justice process will be very different from that of a white woman. Lack of acknowledgement of this in theoretical studies has resulted in decision-makers such as police, judges or magistrates relying on stereotypical assumptions about appropriate behaviour. This chapter thus considers some issues concerning black women which need to be taken into account if they are to have an effective voice in the arena of criminology.

TRADITIONAL APPROACHES

According to Gelsthorpe and Morris the lowest common denominator of feminist perspectives means:

> accepting the view that women experience subordination on the basis of their sex and working towards the elimination of that subordination.[1]

One of the purposes of *feminist criminology*[2] is to consider and advance woman's position so far as understanding crime and criminal justice is concerned. It has not yet fully come to terms with the issues concerning *black women*—possibly due to the strength of white women in the feminist movement. The agenda may not include those items which are most pressing for black women.

Certain studies have sought to distil how women, and women and crime in particular, have historically been perceived (but have not specifically included black women's experiences). In Lucia Zedner's case[3] this was—given the place and period under research—only to be expected. Zedner studied women's prisons in Victorian England and identified links between society's response to crime, prevailing social values and concerns, and its views about women. She focused on the role of gender in relation to social attitudes and responses to criminality, and considered that it was not possible to understand the history of crime or its control in isolation. Thus:

---

[1] *Feminist Perspectives in Criminology*, Gelsthorpe L and Morris A, Open University Press, 1990.

[2] Some people assert that feminist criminology cannot exist as neither *feminism* nor *criminology* are unified sets of principles or practice.

[3] *Women Crime and Custody in Victorian England*, Zedner L, Clarendon Press, 1991.

21

> Changing views of womanhood and women's role in society informed the ways in which criminal women were perceived and treated at every juncture.

Zedner used the example of 'feeble-mindedness', to illustrate how, at the end of the nineteenth century, women were judged as much for moral behaviour as criminal activity. Under the Mental Deficiency Act 1913 those in receipt of poor relief when pregnant or at the time of giving birth could be, and often were, classified as feeble-minded and placed in asylums. Single parent mothers continue to be criticised, yet for many black women single parenthood may be a quite natural state of affairs.

The weakness or frailty—some accounts say evil—of women still prevails in certain accounts of female criminality, thus influencing general perception of the female offender and, more significantly, the offender's perception of herself.

Traditionally, women were either seen as more primitive than men owing to innate biological factors, and therefore less culpable or criminal, or more secretive, dangerous, deceitful or maladjusted. Early observations about female criminality sometimes claimed that women's crimes resulted from their inability to adapt to a natural feminine role. Heidensohn[4], and Morris[5] in their reviews of the literature on female crime identified the following problems:

- women's and girls' crime and deviance were explained more often by biological factors than social or economic forces;
- representations of their motives, or of the circumstances leading to their crimes, were often wrong or distorted; and
- sexual deviance—ranging from a broken hymen to 'immorality' or prostitution—merged with criminal deviance.

Such critiques stemmed from sexist assumptions of predominantly (but not exclusively) male criminologists who tried to explain women's crime, without any real understanding of a woman's perspective.

In recent decades theories have emerged which try to explain the increase in the number of women arrested by reference to claims that female offenders are becoming increasingly more aggressive and

---

[4] *Women and Crime,* Heindesohn F, MacMillan, 1985.
[5] *Women, Crime and Criminal Justice,* Morris A, Basil Blackwell, 1987.

22

violent. Proponents of this kind of view include Freda Adler[6] and Simon[7] who analysed women's arrest trends in the 1960s and early 1970s and put forward ideas about women's criminality (somewhat troubling to feminists) which were largely an extension of the assumption that the emancipation of women depended on achieving legal and social equality with men in public spheres.

Both Adler's and Simon's analyses assumed that female criminality had been kept under control by women's limited aspirations and opportunities. They argued that social circumstances, not biology, explained gender differences in crime. For Adler, the lifting of restrictions on women's behaviour gave them the opportunity to act like men—that is to be as violent, greedy and crime prone as their male counterparts. Simon took a more qualified stance based on her interpretation of the statistical evidence. Having found no changes in women's share of arrest for violent crimes, she reasoned that their increasing share of arrest for property crime (especially larceny, fraud and embezzlement) might be explained by their increasing opportunities in the public sphere to commit crime. Adler has been criticised for claiming a link between the goal of emancipation for women and an increase in female crime and Simon for assuming that such increases were due to new workplace opportunities for some women rather than increasing economic pressures. On a broader front, both have been challenged concerning whether the trends they described were actually occurring.

Roberts,[8] in her study of women and rape, found that until the last two decades little was known about women's experiences, except what filtered through from indirect sources. Where information *had* been collected, for example in wartime, she considered that this was not through concern for women but because it was part of the 'Chronicle of Male Action'. Similarly, Leonard[9] believed that:

> Theoretical criminology is sexist because it unwittingly focuses on the activities, interests and values of men, while ignoring a comparable analysis of women.

---

[6] *Sisters In Crime,* Adler F, McGraw-Hill, New York, 1975.
[7] *Women and Crime,* Simon R J, Lexington, Massachusetts, 1975.
[8] *Women and Rape,* Roberts C, Harvester Wheatsheaf, 1989.
[9] *Women Crime and Society,* Leonard E, Longman, 1982.

TAKING ACCOUNT OF BLACK WOMEN'S EXPERIENCES

The traditional approach described above does not take account of the situation of black women who, for example, have always had to work and function outside conventional roles. In understanding the forces affecting women as a whole it is necessary to acknowledge and incorporate into the debate the complex interconnections between racial, sexual and economic disadvantage and oppression in the lives of black women.

Andrea Canaan, in her essay 'Brownness' describes her experience:

> The fact is I am brown and female, and my growth and development are tied to the entire community. I must nurture and develop brown self, woman, man and child. I must address the issues of my own oppressions and survival. When I separate them, I isolate them, and ignore them, I separate, isolate and ignore myself. I am a unit! A part of brownness.[10]

Just as in trying to speak for all people the law itself ends up silencing those without power, traditional feminist criminology is in danger of silencing certain groups—those who have been kept from speaking, or who have been ignored when they spoke, including black women.

It also has to be recognised that even within minority ethnic communities there are often different responses because experiences of racism, though similar in many ways, have not been identical. Official policies have sometimes had a different impact within or across such communities. African-Caribbeans have mobilised far more around their collective experience of the criminal justice process, particularly of the police and courts, whereas Asian groups have been more actively involved in defending communities against violent attacks, racial harassment, racist immigration laws, and violence against women.[11]

In countries such as Great Britain, the storyteller is usually white, and so 'woman' turns out to be a white woman. In feminist criminology, as in the dominant culture, woman is mostly white and socio-economically privileged. Spelman comments:

---

[10] Cited in Marlee Kline: *Stafford Law Review* 1990.

[11] e.g. Southall Black Sisters represent Asian women's points of view.

24

The real problem has been that feminist theory has confused the condition of one group of women with the condition of all . . . A measure of the depth of white middle-class privilege is that apparently straightforward and logical points and actions at the heart of much of feminist theory guarantee the direction of its attention to the concerns of white middle-class women.[12]

'The family' is, for example, a main cause of contradictory experiences for black women in ways unknown to most white women. Although both black and white women may experience the family as an institution of violence and oppression, for black women it often functions as a source of support against harassment and racism. It provides a cultural and political retreat from white supremacy. Many black women consider their race a more primary factor than gender in their dealings with the criminal justice agencies, such as when the police come to their homes to arrest their children as described in *Chapter 3*.

These different experiences of family life for white women and black women need to be recognised and taken into account. The failure of feminist criminologists to do so and to concentrate on gender oppression is but one illustration of Bell Hooks' observations that:

Certainly it has been easier for women who do not experience race or class oppression to focus exclusively on gender.[13]

The various intersections between race, gender and class oppression—and other differentiating characteristics—affect how and when *all* women experience sexism. They are able to ignore the experience of their race because it does not in any way correlate with an experience of oppression and contradiction. For example, Fry[14] (a white woman) states that white women tend not to think of themselves as white, but merely as women. Thus, it must be recognised that the interests and concerns shared by black women and white women are cut across in a variety of ways by interests of class, sexuality, race and ethnicity.

Lewis[15] accounted for the different crime rates for black and white women, focusing on racism and sexism within the criminal justice process. Sexism had previously been thought to explain the 'chivalry' or leniency shown to women, but Lewis noted that this only included

---

[12] *Inessential Woman*, Spelman E, Beacon Press, Boston, 1988.

[13] *Feminist Theory From Margin to Centre*, Hooks B, South End Press, Boston, 1984.

[14] 1983, USA.

[15] 'Black Women Offenders and Criminal Justice: Some Theoretical Considerations', Lewis D, in *Comparing Female and Male Offenders*, Warren M (Ed.), Sage, 1981, pp.89-105.

those women who adhere to dominant societal gender role expectations. As black women are less often married than white women, more often charged with violent offences, and less 'feminine' in demeanour, they will therefore less often meet such expectations. In addition, Lewis suggests that different personal characteristics may contribute to differences in the nature and extent of crime between black and white women. Black women live in greater relative poverty and both black women and black men are socialised to be independent and assertive. But such characteristics should be viewed with caution, because of the risk of stereotyping black women and ignoring the variations in black communities. They are only useful if they result in a greater understanding of the different roles and expectations of women's behaviour in different cultures. As Kennedy states:

> Until there is a clear appreciation of racism and the social factors which bring black people before the courts, and an understanding of the subtle dynamics which work in the courts to discriminate against them, they will continue to be amongst the sections of the community least well served by the law.[16]

Feminist criminology thus needs to analyse factors such as the disproportionate impact of criminal justice processes on black women, the full effect of race-gender-class on their lives and the perceptions and experiences of black women of the kind relayed in this book.

It must be acknowledged that society's views about different groups of women may come into play in sentencing. Since race affects dominant perceptions of women's 'badness' or 'goodness' it would help to have some information about how black women are viewed (for example by judges and police officers) to determine whether there might be discrimination on the basis of societal perception. It also has to be recognised that behaviour that may be attributed to a 'good' woman in one culture may have the reverse meaning in another. An African woman who arranges with some members of her extended family to care for her children while she spends many hours at the market or finding ways of supporting her children may not be seen in English courts as a 'good' mother who cares for them. It may be that black mothers are considered inadequate by the courts more often than white mothers because they fail to measure up to the dominant (white) ideology of motherhood. Government and media criticism in the 1990s concerning children from single parent families who may become

---

[16] *Eve Was Framed*, Kennedy H, Chatto and Windus, 1992.

delinquent is one example of how dominant values can affect people from minority cultures.

Thus, whilst the ideology of motherhood has dictated that white women stay at home, black women have been regarded as particularly suited for work outside the home, often in someone else's home. For example, African-Caribbean women were encouraged to emigrate to Britain specifically to take positions such as domestics, office cleaners and nurses.[17] At the same time, however, the role of black women as mothers to their own children goes unrecognised and is sometimes actively ignored and discouraged.

Claudia Bernard[18] describes how stereotyping of black mothers as bad parents has strongly influenced these women not to involve the child protection agencies in cases of childhood sexual abuse. Mothers in the study felt vulnerable to implied criticism of their parenting and their capacity to protect their children from abuse. There is over-representation of black (in particular, African-Caribbean) children in the public care system. Also many black women do manual jobs with little pay, and as a result find themselves working even more hours to make ends meet. This can mean spending many hours a day away from their children.

Compared with white women, black women may be affected in more complex and contradictory ways by ideological expectations concerning work and motherhood. This is not to deny that some working class white women find themselves working long hours to make ends meet. Women have to conform to an ideology of motherhood which dictates that mothers should not work outside their homes, especially when children are still young. Black mothers may then be seen as *failed* mothers, precisely because they are single parents, or because their husband or partner has a low wage or is unemployed. The *Census of Population* reports that black women work longer hours compared to white women, and that a greater proportion work full-time.

As Kennedy[19] points out, black mothers often feel their bond with their children is perceived as less significant and that their views on the child's welfare are less valuable. Kennedy cites one mother who was sentenced to two months in prison for refusing access to her daughter's father (a civil matter). She felt that she was viewed as

---

[17] See, generally, *Appendix I* to this work.

[18] 'Childhood Sexual Abuse: The Implications for Black Mothers', Bernard C, *Rights of Women Bulletin*, Winter, 1995.

[19] *Eve Was Framed*, Kennedy H, Chatto and Windus, 1992.

bloody-minded and obstructive, when in fact she was trying to express deep concern for her child's well being. Her ex-boyfriend was a drug user and the little girl returned from visits describing in detail his use of drugs and drug-related involvement with other people. The mother feared that the influence of drugs would affect his ability to care for the child when she was with him, and wanted any access to be supervised. In court her concerns were ignored. She explained:

> The judge thought I was a stubborn determined person who was going out of my way to break a court order. I think had I not had two children by different fathers they would have viewed me as a different type of person. I think the judge was trying to say, you can't have your children and do what you like with them. I think the colour factor comes into it, but it's something that can never be proved.

Many poor women in prison come from run-down housing estates—a problem faced to a greater extent by black women and defined as areas of 'high risk' by the police.[20] The disadvantages which begin to stem from such a lifestyle seem obvious. Throughout there are issues of race, gender and class. For a black woman it is not always easy to know whether the negative response she receives is due to one element or the other, or whether, say, two elements are inter-related. In every black woman's life there are innumerable occasions when she is not only sexually but racially discriminated against.

---

[20] 'Policing of Black Women', Chigwada R, in *Out of Order: Policing of Black People*, Cashmore E and McLaughlin E (Eds.), Routledge, Kegan and Paul, 1986.

Chapter 3

Police and Black Women

In its submission to the Royal Commission on Criminal Procedure in 1992 the Runnymede Trust claimed that racially unequal treatment occurred at all stages of the criminal justice process, from first contact with the police through to imprisonment. Studies of police attitudes from the 1960s to the 1990s have regularly disclosed that racist attitudes are held by many police officers, the 'canteen culture' carrying over from joking with fellow officers to direct encounters with the public. Whilst much has been achieved in recent years—particularly since section 95 Criminal Justice Act 1991 (see *Chapter 1*)—a great deal needs to be done in terms of training, monitoring, working methods and awareness of race and gender issues. Discrimination at the start of the criminal justice process may impact at a later stage, when that discrimination may be compounded by further unequal treatment.

DEVELOPMENTS AND INITIATIVES

In 1995, 2,223 (1.75 per cent) of the 127,222 police officers were from minority ethnic groups, compared with 1.6 per cent in 1989. Thirty-six inspectors, eight chief inspectors and one superintendent were members of minority ethnic groups[1].

In 1993 the Association of Chief Police Officers (ACPO) and the Commission for Racial Equality (CRE) issued a practical guide to all forces entitled 'Policing and Racial Equality'. Police forces have adopted equal opportunities policies and have taken a range of initiatives to develop training on race issues and to increase the recruitment of staff from minority ethnic groups. In addition, Her Majesty's Inspector of Constabulary has produced thematic reports on equal opportunities in 1992 and 1996.

One police force analysed the number of cases in which young people admitted the offence and found that only half as many young Afro-Caribbeans admitted the offence compared to young whites. Cautioning is precluded if the offence is not admitted—and this aspect is perhaps more important than many commentators realise. A suspect

---

[1] 'Race Discrimination and the Criminal Justice System', NAPO, August 1996.

insisting that they are innocent will normally be prosecuted and may be moved up tariff at the sentencing stage, or be given a longer sentence. He or she will also be debarred from any discount for a guilty plea: see, generally, *Chapter 5*.

In 1992, the Commission for Racial Equality (CRE) published a study 'Cautions v. Prosecutions' which examined the decision whether to caution someone or to prosecute them in the courts. This study, in respect of juveniles in seven police force areas, concluded:

> In the majority of forces, proportionately more ethnic minority young people—and particularly Afro-Caribbeans—were referred for prosecution than white young people; in inner city areas the difference was very substantial indeed. The widespread police view that such differentials would indicate that, on average, ethnic minority young people were committing more serious offences was not borne out. Statistical controls for 'offence type' (such as burglary, robbery etc.) suggested that this factor played a very small part in explaining the difference in prosecution rates. Controls for the number of past offences also suggested that this was not the main explanation.

The police are required to conduct ethnic monitoring of stops and searches. In 1996, this was mandatorily extended to *all* police force areas and to arrests, cautions, stop and search and homicide. At the same time, the Crown Prosecution Service (CPS) drew up a sample monitoring scheme for the year 1996-7 involving the random sampling of some 4,000 cases. This exercise involves looking at bail and remand recommendations; charge alteration for a number of specific offences; mode of trial recommendations at court (see, generally, *Chapter 5*); and the discontinuance of prosecutions.

Also in 1996, the Home Office published details of people stopped and searched by the police in 1994-5, broken down by police force area and ethnic group. In England and Wales, 590,918 people were stopped and searched of whom 131,579 (22 per cent) were from minority ethnic groups. The police force with by far the highest proportion of people stopped and searched from minority ethnic groups was the Metropolitan Police with 37 per cent (112,763 out of 302,691).[2]

Activities such as cautioning or stops and searches and their associated policies can be made to seem *discretionary* but are inseparable from any underlying assumptions that blacks commit crimes and that certain types of criminals must be black until shown to be otherwise.

---

[2] Parliamentary answer by David Maclean, Minister of State at the Home Office, to Tim Devlin MP, 29 March 1996.

More recent figures show that the number of black people stopped and searched in London is up to three times greater than would be indicated by the proportion of black people in the general population. Black and ethnic minority citizens are five times more likely to be stopped than white people. Over 25 per cent of all people stopped and searched during 1993 and 1994 were from black and ethnic communities. Virtually all police areas produced stop and search figures where the figure for black people exceeds their level in the general population. Only 10 per cent of all Metropolitan Police stops and searches result in an arrest.[3] A report by the former Greater London Council (GLC) once stated that:

> The police, the courts and the press have combined in the criminalisation of the black community . . . Policing strategy and practice which equates black people with criminals and targets the black community for attention while supported by the racist press results in black people being more likely to arrive in court, to be charged with more serious offences, and thus to have longer criminal records.[4]

The writer and film-maker Roger Graef also found widespread racism amongst police officers he interviewed. He showed that many of them were socialised into a culture 'hostile to all minority groups'. This culture despises blacks, mocking, harassing, abusing and insulting them through the use of crude jokes and offensive nicknames. In an attempt to reassure the interviewer about their prejudices one officer actually said:

> Policemen are insulting about everyone. It's not specially the coons. You hear remarks about poofs, Pakis, lesbos, women, students, the Irish — you name it. We hate everybody.[5]

A further example of racist stereotyping and assumptions is provided by a complaint upheld by the CRE in 1988 after the Staffordshire police distributed a leaflet asking residents to look out for cars being driven by black people and to record the registration numbers. Other studies have shown that, in the Metropolitan Police area, 'blacks' were more likely than whites to be indicted for violent offences, sexual offences and robbery.[6] When cases reached court, a

---

[3] *Runnymede Bulletin*, March 1995.

[4] *Policing London*, Greater London Council, 3,16:17-32, 1985.

[5] *Talking Blues*, Graef R, William Collins and Sons, 1989.

[6] 'The Court Disposals and Remand of White, Afro-Caribbean and Asian Men', Walker M, *British Journal of Criminology*, 29,4: 353-67, 1989.

higher proportion of those involving black people resulted in dismissal because of insufficient evidence (9 per cent as compared with 6 per cent for white people) and a higher proportion of black defendants were acquitted of all indictable offences (15.3 per cent compared with 9.5 per cent). *The Voice* newspaper has pointed out that figures for street crime in Newcastle (mainly populated by white people) suggest that 99.9 per cent of muggings are committed by white youths.

BLACK WOMEN

Without empirical research it is difficult to know whether the racism applied to black men also applies to black women at the same level or for entirely the same reasons. What *is* known is that the police consider black women to be capable of committing crimes in a way the 'normal' or 'good' white women are not.[7] As argued in *Chapter 1*, any such study needs to address issues of race, gender and class and to look at how these inter-relate.

Black women do receive fewer cautions than white women.[8] They are also seven times more likely to be arrested for prostitution than women of other groups.[9] One explanation for the disproportionate number of such arrests may be that economics and class come into play. Black women prostitutes are often forced to practice their profession 'on the streets' instead of under the protection of a benevolent hotel manager or from a luxury apartment, as many white 'working girls' do. A woman's lifestyle can increase the likelihood of police contact, harassment, vulnerability to arrest and risk of involvement in other offences as a result of it carrying her into less safe or more crime prone environments:

> As might be expected, the largest proportion of arrests of black prostitutes takes place in the inner cities where living standards are low, the level of desperation high, and police prejudice endemic.[10]

One study discloses that incarcerated female offenders are more likely than white women to *perceive* the police as excessively brutal,

---

[7] 'Women and Crime in the City', Player E, in *Crime in the City*, Downes D (Ed.), MacMillan, 1989.

[8] 'Race and Criminal Justice', NACRO, 1989.

[9] 'Hustling for Rights', Haft M G, in *The Female Offender*, Crites L (Ed.), Lexington, Massachusetts, 1976: 212

[10] Ibid.

harassing, and unlikely to give them a break through non-arrest.[11] Discretion was exercised more liberally in favour of non-arrest with white women than black women. Moyer and White hypothesise that police officers will apply more severe sanctions to black women than white women, especially if black women are 'loud, boisterous, aggressive, vulgar, and disrespectful'.[12] This is supported by a statement by the Black Women Prison Scheme, an organization which gives moral and material support and visits black women in prison. It is their view that:

> Black women are often seen as violent and that they have to be dealt with by male officers . . . and the officers have been reported to physically rough up these black women in order to prove that they are not like normal white women.

Similarly, the fact that many black women are lone parents can mean that they are viewed in a less favourable way than 'conventional' mothers, and it may bring them into greater contact with the police who, for example, may visit or search their homes looking for young black male suspects. They may also be viewed as 'illegal immigrants.'[13] They may also be too readily assumed to be suffering from mental disorder.

Suspects

A presumption that black people are more likely to commit crime than white people seems to pervade people's thinking in Britain. According to the Penal Affairs Consortium such thinking is misplaced.[14] Black women are the subject of many negative beliefs and attitudes, the victims of racist assumptions which are likely to affect police attitudes towards them. Their sometimes exuberant 'arm-waving' or otherwise excited behaviour may well be misinterpreted.

Common stereotypes afforded to black women include the over-aggressive African woman and the strong, dominant African-Caribbean woman. In contrast, Asian women are viewed as 'passive', 'hysterical', or subject to oppressive practices within the family. Such

---

[11] 'Incarcerated Male and Female Offenders: Perceptions of Their Experiences in the Criminal Justice System', Kratcoski and Scheuerman, *Journal of Criminal Justice*, 2:73-78, 1974; and see 'The Criminalisation and Imprisonment of Black Women', Chigwada R, *Probation Journal*, pp. 100-105, September 1989.

[12] 'Police Processing of Female Offenders', Moyer L and White G F in *Crime in America*, Bowker L (Ed.), MacMillan, New York, 1981.

[13] see under the heading 'Black People and Immigration' later in this chapter.

[14] 'Race and Criminal Justice', Penal Affairs Consortium, September 1996, p.2.

stereotyping has deterred police from taking action or prosecuting in cases of domestic violence involving black women who are seen as able to look after themselves. Helena Kennedy mentions the trial of a Ugandan woman for grievous bodily harm to her husband by pouring hot cooking-fat over him. It came to light that, although she had called the police repeatedly, her violent husband was never arrested. It was suggested to her that she was not telling the truth about making previous complaints. There was no record of the complaints and it was put to her in cross-examination that she was exaggerating her husband's brutality. It was a prosecution witness, a neighbour, who inadvertently came to her aid. He complained in the witness box about the number of times he had been awakened—first by her screams and then by police mistakenly ringing his doorbell when they came in answer to her calls.[15]

In March 1996, the *Runnymede Bulletin* reported the case of a man who died after being sprayed with CS gas. The police were called by the man's wife following a domestic disturbance. Some ten police officers arrived and placed him in a police van. When he developed problems with breathing at the police station he was taken to hospital where he died. The police were called to his home between 4 a.m. and 5 a.m. The man died the same morning at 6.23 a.m. Such events are likely to make other black women involved in domestic violence think twice before calling the police, afraid of what might happen to their partners.

The highly-publicised case of Joy Gardner, a black woman of Jamaican origin who died in 1993 in London, lends support to the view that black women can be seen by the authorities as potentially violent. Joy Gardner had overstayed her visa and was visited by the Alien Deportation Group. Her wrists were handcuffed to a leather strap around her waist, bound by a second belt around her thighs, and a third one around her ankles. As she lay on the floor, 13 feet of adhesive tape was wound around her head and face. Mrs. Gardner collapsed, and died in hospital a few hours later. Until her tragic death the use of body belts, surgical tape and the existence of a special deportation squad was unknown to the general public. It subsequently came to light that two other African women had been deported in this way.

If Joy Gardner had been an Australian or a New Zealander the police and immigration authorities are most unlikely to have found it necessary to send so many officers to her house, nor would they have used such methods. What underlies the events is the perception of

---

[15] *Eve Was Framed*, Kennedy H, Chatto and Windus, 1992.

black women as aggressive. There would have been horror in white suburbia if a middle-class white woman had been treated in the way Joy Gardner was—and it seems almost inconceivable that she would have been 'taped up' in such a fashion.

Three officers were tried for the murder of Joy Gardner and acquitted. In effect, the trial put the victim in the dock. As if to honour the standard stereotype and myth of the 'big strong black woman', she was described by one of the officers as '. . . the strongest and most violent woman' he had ever encountered. One of the officers said that the treatment she received was 'reasonable in all the circumstances'. Some politicians used the events to hammer home their anti-black, anti-refugee message. Teresa Gorman, conservative MP for Billericay, said:

> She had been bumming on the Social Services for five years . . . she had cost the taxpayer an enormous amount . . . if she had gone quietly none of this would have happened. [16]

This stereotype that black women are inherently more aggressive is unfounded. On the contrary, most of them are subdued at the shock of first-time contact with the criminal justice agencies and, in the case of foreign women, the relative strangeness of British culture.

Just as the police may regard black women as suspects because of the assumptions they make about their lifestyle, the way they are portrayed by the media also affects matters. Overall, they are labelled 'deviant' because they are do not conform to what British society conceives to be 'correct behaviour' and they are powerless to protest in individual cases because of their class, economic status or lack of social position. The following press report is indicative:

> Young black men commit a disproportionately high number of violent crimes in London because most black mothers, when they are young girls, have children out of wedlock and are not supported by the fathers. There appears to be less stigma attached to single parenthood in the black community. The only hope is that somehow the West Indian marriage can be encouraged and supported. [17]

The implications are that black women, as single parents, deviate from the norm and in so doing are to blame for the criminality of their

---

[16] *NMP Annual Report* 1995/96.
[17] *London Evening Standard*, 12 December 1987.

young men. As far back as 1973, it was reported that the Broadwater Farm Estate in North London was occupied by:

> Problem families and the sight of unmarried West Indian mothers walking about the estate aggravated racial tensions.[18].

Such reports only serve to criminalise black women and to reinforce beliefs that the home environment—especially their style of parenting and mothering—is to blame, something which may also be coloured by thoughts of loose sexual practices.

Visher has suggested that lenient or harsh treatment by law-enforcement agencies at any stage of the process depends on the degree to which a woman's behaviour is in accordance or at variance with the female role. This research concluded that chivalrous treatment at the arrest stage depended upon a larger set of gender expectations that exist between men and women in their encounters with police-officers and that '. . . those female suspects who violate typical middle-class standards of traditional female characteristics and behaviour (i.e. white, older and submissive) are not afforded any chivalrous treatment in arrest decisions'.[19] Other researchers have made similar points, arguing that '. . . the processual consequences of stereotypes not only shape public attitudes and behaviour towards deviants, but guide the very choice of individuals who are to be so defined and processed.'[20]

THREE SCENARIOS

The Newham Monitoring Project (NMP) has documented a number of real-life cases (anonymised for the purposes of this book but all three occurring in the 1990s) which illustrate the type of situation which this chapter has sought to convey:

Mrs. A
Police officers visited the home of Mrs. A, an elderly black woman, to arrest her son. The police mistakenly attempted to arrest Richard in the belief that he was Richard's brother Jason. Both Richard and his mother tried to explain the misunderstanding but the officers forced their way into the house and pulled Richard out, allegedly beating him

---

[18] *Hornsey Journal,* 11 May 1973.

[19] 'Gender, Police Arrest Decisions and Notions of Chivalry', Visher C, *Criminology,* 21:5-27, 1983

[20] *Deviance and Social Control,* Swigert V L and Farrel R A, Glenview, University of Illinois Press, 1977.

in the process and pushing his mother heavily in the chest, causing her to collapse with severe chest pains. It is said that if it was not for the swift action of her children Mrs. A could have died. Mrs. A was admitted to hospital and was there for five days. She and her son sued the police and, in an out of court settlement, obtained £28,000 in lieu of damages for assault, wrongful arrest and false imprisonment. They also won an apology from the police, but so far as is known, no disciplinary action has been taken against the officers concerned.

Mrs. B

Mrs. B died when police went to her house to arrest her son. She was shot by the police. At the inquest, a verdict of accidental death was returned, thereby absolving the police but, seemingly, vindicating her family's case that the police search contributed directly to the heart attack which killed her. Again, no disciplinary action was taken.

Mrs. C

The case of Mrs. C illustrates how police actions can quickly turn a criminal investigation involving a black woman into an immigration issue. Mr. and Mrs. C lived on an estate. From the day they moved into their first floor maisonette, they were subjected to racial harassment from their white neighbours in a notoriously hostile part of London. One evening, whilst Mrs. C was relaxing in her front room, her three young children aged three and two were out playing on the balcony with her three month old baby in his pram. Mrs. C said that the children were at no time left unattended, as the front door was open, enabling her to keep a close eye on them. Mr. C was at work.

The two-year-old, who had a pedal car, climbed onto it and reached up, thus managing to hang his head over the balcony. Immediately Mrs. C saw this, she ran out and shouted at him to get down in her strong Jamaican accent. Her neighbours understood this to mean that she was going to throw the child over the balcony. Within minutes, whilst Mrs. C was still outside calming the children down, she saw a police van driving up close to her home. A few seconds later, three male police officers walked straight into her home without invitation, as her front door was still open. Mrs. C said she felt intimidated and humiliated by the audacity of the officers, whose form of greeting was to tell her that they had come out in response to her neighbour's report that she was drunk and attempting to throw her son over the balcony. Mrs. C, taken aback by what the officers said, became distressed. She could not understand the policemen's view of this information. They did not, she said, even believe that she was the mother of the children. She had to prove this by producing their birth certificates. The officers then asked Mrs. C to produce her passport to show what her immigration status was. When she said that her passport was in a suitcase in an upstairs bedroom, she was followed up the stairs by all three officers. Whilst her passport was checked, Mrs. C was repeatedly warned that even though she was a *legal* immigrant, she could still be deported and have her children taken away from her. At that point, she broke down in tears, triggering an extraordinary response from the police. They began to ransack Mrs. C's drawers and picked up her pants, holding these up to her and asking who she wore them for. Mrs. C was not only stripped of her dignity, but as she later told an NMP worker, she was terrified and felt '. . . like I had been raped'.

Mrs. C was told to go downstairs as the officers were taking her and the children to the police station. She was not allowed to clothe or prepare a feed for her three-month-old son before leaving. This was on a cold evening in March. The police officers later said they did that '. . . to ensure the safety and well-being of the children'. Mrs. C was denied the right to make a phone call to her husband, or to hold her baby until she was seated in the police van—where, according to Mrs. C, her young son was 'literally hurled' at her.

At the police station, Mrs. C and her three young children were put in a cell and left until a duty social worker arrived. The social worker was so alarmed by the way she had been treated that she gave her NMP's emergency telephone. After another three hours Mrs. C's husband was finally contacted and told that his family had been removed from their home because there were concerns for the safety of the children .

Mrs. C was released without charge and never given a satisfactory explanation. The following morning, Mr. and Mrs. C contacted NMP for help and NMP contacted the local Social Services Department to find out what, if anything, they knew about the case. The response was that the Social Services department had been contacted by the Child Protection Team, but had expressed serious concerns about the way in which young children were being removed from their homes in the absence of a social worker. The police, however, insisted that this was part of a 'joint' case between themselves and the social services.

In the hope that she would get some recompense, Mrs. C put in a formal complaint. The officers concerned denied all her allegations. The Police Complaints Authority (PCA) came up with what now appears to be a standard response. In a letter, Mrs. C was told that '. . . there were no other witnesses to this incident and therefore no means of reconciling the conflicting accounts given. Having carefully studied all the papers contained in the report of the investigation, the Authority have decided that no formal disciplinary action should be taken'. The incident left Mrs. C deeply traumatised, so that she had to be put on tranquillisers. As a result, she was not alert for a while, and she could not properly look after her children. During that period, her husband had to take indefinite leave from work to care for his family. Mr. C's employers were becoming impatient with him and threatened to sack him.

As a result of the incident it is said that the C family became isolated and the development of the three-year-old's speech more impaired, as he was afraid to go out and play with other children. The experience almost tore the family apart. Fortunately, Mrs. C's children were not placed on the local 'at risk' register (another indication that there was no significant problem had the police investigated the matter more thoroughly rather than making assumptions). Instead, Mrs. C was assigned the support of a home help during what was a difficult period. Even after a year, she was still feeling insecure and nervous.

Other cases

After the Brixton riots and the Broadwater Farm riots, black women lived in fear of being separated from their children, either if they, themselves, were arrested (with the likelihood that their young children would be left alone), or if their older children were arrested.[21] Police officers, in many instances armed, visited over 1,000 homes on the Broadwater Farm Estate after the riots and an indication of the fear that such visits caused is provided by the testimony of one black mother:

> They (the police) said that he (her son) had been picked up for the murder of the policeman, and it would be better for him if I told them everything I knew about what he was doing on the night of the riot. When I said my son didn't know anything about the murder they called me a 'stupid bitch' and refused to let me see him. I never had any quarrel with the police, but now I lie awake at night worrying in case the boys have been picked up again.[22]

---

[21] *The Women of Broadwater Farm,* Local Pamphlet (and see next footnote), 1989.

[22] 'Return of Broadwater Farm', Platt S, *New Socialist,* April 1986.

BLACK PEOPLE AND IMMIGRATION

Black women's experiences of policing are quite often bound up with Britain's immigration and nationality laws. These laws have undergone considerable refinement and expansion in the post-war period, but as Paul Gordon has argued, they have not simply been concerned with controlling who has a right of entry to Britain. 'Immigration control has increasingly entailed the growth of controls and surveillance of those (black people) already here. To this end, the police and the immigration services have been given ever-increasing resources, both in terms of personnel and technology.'[23] Such powers and resources have resulted in the police stopping and questioning black people about their nationality as well as conducting controversial passport raids on black communities.[24] Gordon argues that *all* black people are seen as immigrants. Given that some are illegal, it is common to hear comments such as 'The only way to tell an illegal black from a legal one is to suspect the lot'. This has led many black people not to report any crime to the police for fear of it being turned into an immigration enquiry. A case reported in *The Guardian* supports this view.[25] A 29-year-old black man of Nigerian parentage but born in the United Kingdom went to a police station in South London in July 1993 to report the theft of his fiancé's car radio. He was arrested and detained for more than three hours after police questioned him about his immigration status. Police took him in handcuffs to his home, where he showed them his passport and birth certificate. He was taken back to the police-station, fingerprinted and detained for another one and a half hours. He was not believed when he told police officers that he was born in this country. He sued for false imprisonment, assault and discrimination under the Race Relations Act. He achieved an undisclosed but 'substantial' out-of-court settlement.

Robert Reiner explains how black people are seen as immigrants. Police officers were found to suspect someone of being an illegal immigrant only in the case of black people. He contrasts two scenarios to make the point. A middle-aged, very respectably dressed, politely mannered, black doctor born in Africa was stopped by a police officer on suspicion that his road fund licence (tax disc) was out-of-date, which it turned out not to be. However, the officer's suspicions were aroused by his driving documents. The doctor was called Mohammed

---

[23] *Policing Immigration: Britain's Internal Controls*, Gordon P, Pluto, 1985.

[24] Institute of Race Relations, 1979: 13-17.

[25] 17 March 95.

aroused by his driving documents. The doctor was called Mohammed Ali (itself a cause of mirth and some ribaldry: it being also that of a former World Heavyweight Boxing Champion), but whereas one document referred to Mohammed Ali, another referred to Ali Mohammed. On this somewhat slender basis he was brought in 'for questioning.'

His bad luck was compounded by the fact that the custody officer that night was Sergeant 'Cynic'—'the personification of the most bigoted aspects of canteen culture found in police studies.' Sergeant Cynic put the doctor through the booking-in ritual, peppered by provocative remarks When he heard the suspect was a doctor he sneered, 'Where is your degree from, Addis Ababa?', to which the doctor responded coolly 'No, Edinburgh University '. The doctor retained a polite, calm, but not deferential demeanour throughout all this. Reiner states that he subsequently learned that he had been held for nearly 24 hours before being totally vindicated by immigration officials.

The contrasting case Reiner gives is one of the arrest of a white American student in his late twenties who had been found urinating in the street. He was very drunk and rude, cursing at the officers and threatening to sue them. His manners were quintessential of the kind which the literature suggests would normally result in having the book thrown at you. There was an extended legal discussion subsequently between the arresting officer, custody officer and duty inspector to find the most serious possible charge, but what was remarkable, Reiner adds, was the failure to even consider that he might be in breach of his residence conditions. He purported to be a student, but had been here for eight years, and had no scholarship or legitimate means of support apart from 'a rich dad'! The police officers accepted this explanation without question.

Reiner says that it certainly occurred to him, as a mere observer, that the student might be working, in a legitimate or illegitimate occupation, but at any rate in breach of his landing conditions. Yet this quite obvious possibility was never raised, let alone investigated by the officers, despite their eagerness to 'get' him.[26]

The problem of the use and abuse of immigration powers in relation to black women was also highlighted by a case reported in *Campaign Against Racism and Fascism*[27] in which an East African woman

---

[26] *Race, Crime and Justice: Models of Interpretation in Minority Ethnic Groups in the Criminal Justice System*, Reiner R, Cambridge University Institute of Criminology, Cropwood Conference Series, No. 21, 1992.

[27] Issue No. 7, 1978.

who stopped to ask a policewoman for directions was held at the police-station until her passport could be produced. In a 1989 case, a police officer called at the home of a Nigerian woman under the guise of checking her immigration status, which was in fact legal. He threatened her with deportation and demanded sexual favours as insurance against this. Eventually, the woman was awarded £8,000 in damages with the judge stating that the police officer had '. . . acted behind the shadow of the warrant card and the strength of the law for his own squalid purposes'.[28]

In another case , a black woman was taken to the police station by police officers who had come to her flat to look for her partner. After the police had searched the house and found nothing, they took the woman with them to the police station 'to answer questions about a forged passport'. When she pointed out that the picture on the forged passport bore no resemblance to her, the officers said: 'We know you black people, you disguise yourselves'. The police used family responsibilities to force a 'confession' out of her. She was further victimised in that she was not told of her rights and was not seen by a solicitor. On the second day of the hearing, the passport charge was dropped.[29]

MENTAL HEALTH POWERS

Section 136 Mental Health Act 1983 covers situations where a person's behaviour is causing a nuisance or offence. Incidents leading to the use of the section are usually reported to the police by members of the public and routinely involve minor offences. The provision reads:

> If a constable finds in a public place to which the public have access a person who appears to him to be suffering from mental disorder and to be in immediate need of care or control, the constable may, if he thinks it necessary to do so in the interests of that person or for the protection of other persons, remove that person to a place of safety.

Somebody removed under section 136 can be detained at a 'place of safety' for up to 72 hours. The intention behind the provisions is to ensure that 'mentally disordered' people are examined by a registered medical practitioner and interviewed by an approved social worker so as to make arrangements for their care. It is the only provision in the

---

[28] *The Times*, 1 August 1989.

[29] 'The Criminalisation and Imprisonment of Black Women', Chigwada R, *Probation Journal*, 1989, pp. 100-105.

without medical evidence, to deprive someone of his or her liberty. The appropriateness of police involvement in medical issues and the use of police vans instead of ambulances has been questioned by organisations such as the National Association for Mental Health (MIND).

The statutory definition of 'place of safety' includes a police station. (Given the history of deaths in police custody, the designation of the police station as a 'place of safety' seems somewhat ironic). As Faulkner has argued:

> Section 136 of the Mental Health Act is essentially a way of dealing with situations that cannot be dealt with by direct recourse to the mental health social services. As such, it is a necessary inclusion in the Act. However, the procedure followed in London (where the section is most frequently used) gives the police greater power with which to detain and refer people, as a result of which both men and women tend to be admitted to hospital for three days following police detention, and are rarely assessed by social workers. [30]

Other studies have shown that young African-Caribbean immigrants are up to 25 times more likely than white people to be committed for detention under Part III of the Mental Health Act 1983, [31] and that African-Caribbean people born in Britain were admitted at four times the rate for whites. [32] Browne examined the extent to which black people are remanded for psychiatric reports when appearing before magistrates' courts, the nature and outcome of psychiatric remands, and the implications for the provision of services to black people who have passed through the psychiatric remand process. He found that 36 (32 per cent) of the people given hospital orders without restrictions were known to be black. [33] Further evidence is provided by studies examining mental illness rates for black people within the community. More generally, The mental hospital admission rate for people born in England and Wales was 494 per 100,000 whilst the rate for the Caribbean-born community was 539 and the number of first admissions for schizophrenia among black people was three times the norm. Dr. S. P. Sashidhartam commented in *The Guardian*:

---

[30] 'Women and Section 136 of the Mental Health Act 1983', Faulkner A, in *The Boys in Blue,* Dunhill C (Ed.), Virago, 1989.

[31] Wards, 1992.

[32] 'The Compulsory Detention of Afro-Caribbeans under the Mental Health Act', Cope R, *New Community,* 1989, April: 343-356.

[33] 'Black People, Mental Health and the Courts', Browne D, NACRO, 1990.

> The crisis in British psychiatry is not about large numbers of black people breaking down with any given psychiatric diagnosis, but how such individuals are being inducted into the mental health services and being labelled as having serious mental illness.[34]

The possibility that high rates of police admissions may be partly affected by conscious or unconscious racist attitudes has been a cause of concern among psychiatrists. Writing about his clinical experiences in the East End of London, Littlewood and Lipsedge stated that it was 'certainly true' that the police could be behaving in an overtly racist manner as an alternative to arrest, selectively picking out mentally healthy black people and taking them to psychiatric hospitals under section 136.[35]

Dunn and Fahy compared emergency police referrals of black people and white people to an urban psychiatric hospital based in a catchment area with a large African-Caribbean population. They attempted to establish whether rates of the referral of blacks were different from those for whites, to ascertain the ability of the police to identify mental disorder among different ethnic groups, and to examine the reasons for referral and the outcome of admission among ethnic groups.[36]

There were 268 referrals during the period of their study. Amongst this number 165 (61 per cent) were white and 88 (33 per cent) were black. The majority of the patients had a previous psychiatric history: 73 per cent of white men and 67 per cent of black men had a history of psychiatric admission, in comparison with 87 per cent of white women and 92 per cent of black women. The proportions admitted under section 136 previously were 40 per cent for white women and 32 per cent for black women. Schizophrenia was the commonest diagnosis in all groups, but was made twice as often in blacks as whites. Personality disorder and alcohol and drug-abuse were more commonly diagnosed in white patients and drug-induced psychosis was more frequently diagnosed in black men.

The study also found that black people were more likely to receive psychotropic medication, especially neuroleptics: 90 per cent of black men as opposed to 63 per cent of white men, and 83 per cent of black

---

[34] 4 November 1989.

[35] *Transcultural Psychiatry,* Littlewood R and Lipsedge M, Churchill-Livingstone, 1979.

[36] 'Police Admissions to Psychiatric Hospital: Demographic and Clinical Differences Between Ethnic Groups', Dunn J and Fahy T A, *British Journal of Psychiatry,* 1990, 156: 373-378.

women as opposed to 80 per cent of white women. Furthermore, 88 per cent of black men were kept in hospital after the section 136 order had lapsed as opposed to 74 per cent of white men, and 81 per cent of black women as opposed to 73 per cent of white women. Black men (48 per cent) were also more likely to be offered follow-up treatment than white men (25 per cent), as were black women (71 per cent) when compared with white women (58 per cent).

It is also clear from this study that more black women than white women were referred by the police to mental hospitals under section 136. This finding is supported by a Police Monitoring and Research Group study which found that many more black women than white women were detained in police stations or taken to mental hospitals under this section.[37] Again, because black women tend to speak loudly and are from a different cultural background their behaviour tends to be misinterpreted and this can result in their being seen as 'crazy' or in need of psychiatric help. MIND found that in a minority of cases the police breached the conditions of section 136 by removing people, mainly women, from their own or other peoples homes. Black women could be particularly vulnerable to such breaches. In neighbourhood disputes police tend to take a black woman to the police station or other 'place of safety' if the neighbourhood is white. If the neighbours are both black the police tend to take no action.

There are serious ramifications in being sent to a psychiatric hospital under section 136. The period of detention can be indefinite, the patient is under constant observation and 'good behaviour' can mean patients submitting their rights to the ward staff. If a patient tries to assert his or her rights he or she may be labelled as 'disturbed' and this may further prolong the stay. Doctors and nurses have the right to give drugs to a patient against his or her will and the effects of some psychotropic drugs (e.g. Haloperidol and Largactil), which may be given in high doses to black people, have serious side effects. Some people end up walking with difficulty (sometimes called 'Largactil shuffle') or like a zombie. Once taken to a 'place of safety', psychiatrists tend to diagnose black women and working-class women as suffering from 'psychosis', rather than 'neurosis', which is the preferred diagnosis for white middle-class women. Such labelling in police records may adversely affect a woman's future involvement with the criminal justice process as well as negatively impacting upon other aspects of her life.

---

[37] 1987, No. 26.

MIND found that a large number of black women 'sectioned' due to police action were later diagnosed as 'not mentally ill' at the hospital. More women are detained under section 136 than for criminal charges (this may be instead of being charged of course) and their rights are limited. Under section 136 there is no right to see a solicitor and any children may be taken into the care of the local authority. If employed, an individual's job may also be jeopardised. Another problem under this provision is that if a woman is not diagnosed as in need of hospital treatment, but released after the 72 hours allowed by the Act for detention, she has no redress in law, unless she can prove that the police acted 'in bad faith or without reasonable care.'

INTERVIEWS

Over two-thirds of the women who were interviewed claimed that they had been 'manhandled' by the police at one time or another. One women, speaking of her experience at the police station, said:

> Police officers look at you and talk to you like you are not a human being. They do not know how to handle people and have a bad attitude . . . There are some nice officers but the majority are horrible. (Dawn)

> Police were horrible to me. They refused me to speak to a solicitor. (Aisha)

> Police think all black people are criminals. They see us as suspects and stop you. (Karen)

The women talked about their other experiences with the police:

> I got arrested at work at the post office by the investigating squad. I had cashed a pension book. The police refused me to make a phone call to my mother to pick up my daughter from nursery. (Monica)

> The police were threatening me with all sort of things when I was in police custody. (Karen)

> Police officers seem to think most black people cannot write or read. I told them I can write myself. (Maxine)

The women thus had a negative view of the police, felt that they had been ill-treated because they were black, and that police attitudes to black women are unhelpful. When considering complaints from black people, black people may be viewed as suffering from some kind of paranoia. The women also felt that the police sometimes exceed their rights. Marva stated that:

> I got searched in the office. When the police went to my flat they were saying that everything in my flat was proceeds of crime. They turned my house upside down.

Lorraine who was pregnant at the time of arrest said that:

> The police pushed me about and took me to the police station with my brother's girlfriend who was also pregnant. Whilst in the police cell, the police went back to my flat broke the door and searched the flat . . . There was no need for that . . . they could have asked me for the keys. They found nothing but took my filofax, baby clothes and photographs. It was wrong for them to do that. I should have been present. I did not know about all this until the next day. They would not treat a pregnant white woman like that.

Some of the women complained about the state of the police cell. Dorothy said:

> The cell was really . . . You couldn't put your dog in there. I said to them do you expect me to stay in this crap . . . I said I am not staying in here and just put my finger on the buzzer. I rang it for about an hour and refused to take my finger off . . . I said unless you put me in the detention centre which was much better. In this cell, men had . . . on the wall.

Only Alithea, who had a criminal record from the age of 13, had anything favourable to say:

> I have nothing bad to say about the police. I would say it depends on your attitude. They have been professional with me and I am always co-operative and it makes life easier for everyone.

Police officers have been known to take no action if the person responds well to them and respectfully. The way a woman is dressed seems to matter. Police officers in Elaine Player's research stated that '. . . they would be more likely to arrest a woman who behaved aggressively or who was verbally abusive or obstructive than a woman who was trying to be helpful or appeared to regret what she had done.'[38] But it can also be pointed out that the way the police treat and

---

[38] 'Women and Crime in the City', Player E, in *Crime in the City*, Downes D (Ed.), Macmillan, 1989.

speak to black women may contribute to the way black women respond to them. Rhona, who had been in trouble with the police a few times, said:

> I feel that black people are persecuted for no reason at all. They can stop you, interrogate you and if they are not satisfied they will arrest you. They will ask you questions like . . . where do you get your money from? Where do you live? and they will ask you . . . Can you read and write? They assume all black people are illiterates.

The women also felt that some police and customs officers take cases personally so that if charges are not brought this seems to reflect failure on their part. In Beatrice's case (see *Chapter 6*), for example, the prosecutor took the relatively unusual step of obtaining a voluntary bill of indictment for her trial at the Crown Court after the magistrates' court found that there was *insufficient evidence* to commit the matter for trial by jury:

> The customs officers in my case are taking the case personally. Its like they want us to be found guilty even though they have no evidence. (Beatrice)

COMMENT

At the very least, this chapter discloses a need for further training if police officers are to understand other cultures and stop racist and sexist behaviour and attitudes towards black women. This is not to say that black women do not commit crimes, but that wrong conclusions are often drawn from their lifestyles and modes of behaviour, and that racism plays a significant part in the extent to which black women are stopped, searched, cautioned, charged, prosecuted, held in custody or taken to mental hospitals. Those initiatives by the police and CPS described at the beginning of this chapter are to be welcomed as a first step, but all initiatives and training need to take account of the hitherto neglected topic of black *women*.

Chapter 4

Probation and Black Women

Considerable advances have been made in the 1990s in the way that the probation service confronts discrimination and discriminatory practices. The preparation of pre-sentence reports (PSRs)—the single most important aspect of the work of the probation service in so far as day-to-day decision making by the criminal courts is concerned— is governed (as is much other probation work) by National Standards. This requires, among other items of good and effective practice, that PSRs are free of discrimination on the grounds of race, gender, age, disability, language, ability, literacy, religion and sexual orientation. All probation service areas must have a clear equal opportunities policy with a built-in review and monitoring system. Similar principals affect the provision by the probation service of community sentences (probation orders and community service) and the work of the probation service in prisons and when supervising offenders under the modern scheme for early release from prison whereby ex-prisoners except those serving terms of less than six months remain under the supervision of a probation officer until the expiry of the term of their original sentence.

Under the original version of the Criminal Justice Act 1991, a written PSR had to be considered before certain sentences were imposed, i.e. custody (except where the court considered the PSR to be unnecessary in relation to indictable only cases, i.e. those very serious offences which by law can only be tried in the Crown Court, or where the sentence is fixed by law, e.g. life imprisonment for murder) and the more demanding community sentences. This was altered by the Criminal Justice and Public Order Act 1994 and courts were given a general discretion to dispense with a PSR where they deem one to be unnecessary (provisions still apply where the offender is below 18 years of age to ensure a PSR in most instances). The effect has been to return a discretion to courts, and other comments in this work concerning the scope for discrimination whenever such a discretion exists (see. e.g. *Chapter 3* in relation to decisions by the police whether to caution or arrest) apply equally to this aspect of the criminal justice process. Stereotypes and assumptions about black women need to be avoided, as do beliefs e.g. that they are more crime prone or likely to re-offend which are not supported by the data. A main focus of the PSR is the seriousness of the offence, the risk to the public where the offence is a sexual or violent one, and the risk of re-offending, thereby reflecting the considerations for courts discussed in *Chapter 5*.

The professional organizations involved in the probation service— principally the Association of Chief Probation Officers (ACOP), the National Association of Probation Officers (NAPO) and the Association of Black Probation Officers (ABPO) have all taken steps to promote racial equality in every aspect of the service's work, including the production of policy statements and practice guidance. Similarly, area probation services have, as required, produced equal opportunities policy statements, and for example given special responsibility for race relations to staff of chief officer grade, introduced monitoring of PSRs and other reports to courts and other areas of practice designed to ensure that they are non-discriminatory.[1]

In March 1995, 585 of the 7,905 probation officers (7.6 per cent) were from minority ethnic groups, compared to 2.6 per cent in 1989. The number of senior probation officers from such groups has risen from three to 42 (0.26 per cent to 3.4 per cent). In March 1995, eight members of minority ethnic groups were in management positions in the service, none of whom were chief probation officers.[2]

Probation officers are trained in social work practice and acquire skills which enable them to challenge attitudes and behaviour which result in crime and which cause distress to victims, but it also seeks:

at all times to bring out the best in people . . . reconciling offenders and communities, recognising the obligation of both.[3]

Notwithstanding the duty to avoid discrimination there is a constant need for vigilance. Acknowledging that improved practices have since been developed, research indicates that black offenders are less likely than their white counterparts to be made the subject of a probation order.[4] Proportionately more PSRs or medical reports are requested on women.[5] The courts are more likely to ask for a report on

---

[1] An outline of the work of the probation service, its history and the changing nature of its work from an essentially social work agency to one charged with a more pragmatic role in relation to offenders, is contained in *Introduction to the Probation Service*, Osler, Waterside Press, 1995.

[2] 'Race, Discrimination and the Criminal Justice System', NAPO and ABPO, August 1996.

[3] Probation Service Statement of Purpose, Home Office 1992.

[4] 'Racism and Criminology: Concepts and Controversies', Hudson B in Racism and Criminology, Cook D and Hudson B (Eds.), 1993.

[5] 'Female Offenders and the Probation Service', Mair G and Brockington N, Howard Journal, Vol 27, No. 2, May 1988, pp. 117-126.

a first offender when that offender is a woman.[6] But, seemingly, this does not apply in the case of foreign black women where there are only limited efforts to obtain information from abroad.

Since the Criminal Justice Act 1991, PSRs seek to give information about possible community sentence provision in the light of the facts of the offence. The very fact that a PSR is prepared may have an effect, such as increasing the likelihood of a community sentence, but the effect can also be an adverse one in the sense that, in the mind of the court, the very existence of a PSR can give an impression of greater seriousness or concern about the offender. Carefully thought out 'gatekeeping' strategies seek to guard against this and various attempts have been made to agree seriousness scales with courts so that reports are only required in appropriate cases and probation officers deal with their enquiries in the light of some understanding of the court's intentions in the matter. There has been a shift away from welfare considerations (the former social inquiry report often contained considerable detail about an offender's personal background and history) towards offence based considerations. Immediately ahead of the introduction of the present system, the need for welfare-based intervention was identified as a significant factor in relation to a large number of women given probation orders for minor and first offences.[7]

Commenting on the state of the research and a Home Office study 'Sentencing Practice in the Crown Court'[8], the Penal Affairs Consortium noted in September 1996 that:

> . . . There was . . . a highly significant and disturbing difference in the extent to which social inquiry reports (SIRs) were prepared on different ethnic groups . . . 22 per cent of white defendants had no SIR compared with 37 per cent of black and Asian defendants. Part of the reason for this difference stemmed from differences in relation to plea. Eighteen per cent of whites, 24 per cent of Asians and 20 per cent of black defendants pleaded 'not guilty' and reports were prepared in 51 per cent of contested cases compared with 82 per cent of guilty plea cases. However, substantial differences remained in the extent to which reports were provided for different racial groups after allowing for plea.[9]

---

[6] Women Offenders in Merseyside, Humphreys B, Merseyside Probation Service, Edmunds, 1993.

[7] H. M. Inspectorate of Probation Report, 1991.

[8] 'Sentencing Practice in the Crown Court', Moxon D, Home Office Research Study No 103, Home Office, 1988.

[9] 'Race and Criminal Justice', Penal Affairs Consortium, September 1996.

The consortium also expressed concern that women convicted of minor offences are more likely to receive probation in circumstances where men receive lesser sentences.[10] In appropriate circumstances, community sentences, including probation orders, are important in that they allow a woman to serve her sentence hopefully doing something constructive and looking after her family. Any children will not have to be taken from the mother and placed in local authority care or accommodation. They will not suffer 'secondary punishment' for a crime they, the children, did not commit. Also, if a woman is placed on probation she will not risk losing her flat (often a council flat) or job, and she will escape the label that attaches to an ex-prisoner (see, generally, *Chapter 8*). People who go to prison tend to come out more knowledgeable about crime and how to commit it.

Probation orders may be used as an alternative to imprisonment for white defendants, but for black women they may equally be used as an alternative to a discharge, fine or some other lesser punishment, thereby limiting the scope for community sentences in the future. There is a case for arguing for a greater use of probation and other community sentences for women, few of whom are in prison for violent crimes or other offences which seriously threaten the community. As this book has sought to explain in other chapters, in this regard there is nothing other than the misleading myth of the black woman as aggressive or inherently violent to make courts behave differently towards them.

There are themes common to the Probation Service and other social work agencies which are particularly relevant to women users. Gelsthorpe indicated that administrative and organizational factors, as opposed to fixed assumptions, were responsible for girls and boys being treated differently by criminal justice agencies. Social work has traditionally defined women primarily in relation to their families and particularly in their capacity as mothers and by holding them responsible for maintaining family harmony. Women may be prevented from making their own choices and are maintained in roles dependent on others.[11] All such matters have a heightened effect in the case of black women who may deviate from normal expectations as has been outlined in *Chapters 1* and *2*.

The work of the Probation Service as recounted by King[12] and Osler[13] indicates that, *historically* speaking, its work centres on male

---

[10] Ibid.

[11] *Sexism and the Female Offender: An Organisational Analysis*, Gelsthorpe L, Gower, Cambridge Studies in Criminology, 1989.

[12] *The Probation Service*, King J, Butterworths, 1958.

offenders. In her third edition, published in 1969, King continued to describe *all* offenders as men. References to women locate them in the home with family responsibilities and no reference is made to women in discussions of through-care, hostels, employment, drug addiction or, even more surprisingly, psychiatric help. In 1990, the National Association of Probation Officers identified in its practice guidelines the need to challenge traditional attitudes towards women and cautions against assumptions that women and black clients are 'more difficult' and present more problems than white male clients.

Studies of a qualitative nature have looked at references in PSRs and analysed the frames of reference within which they occur. Whitehouse's 1982 study showed how racism can surface in the work of the probation service. He looked at racial bias in social inquiry reports (the precursor of the PSR). It started from the premise that the cause of black people being unequally represented in various categories of supervision is the cumulative effect of racial disadvantage and the lack of available sentencing options for black people. The disadvantage thus begins, Whitehouse argues, at the referral stage for reports. It continues via the proportion of recommendations for probation and in the concurrence between recommendations and the sentence of the court. Such findings are relevant to the situation of black women and the way they are perceived by the criminal justice process as a whole, of which the work of the probation service in responding to the requirements of other agencies or the process set in train by them is just a part. Whitehouse examined the qualitative nature of descriptive material in SIRs and noted that social work practice is dominated by the values of the dominant culture (see the general comments in *Chapter 1* of this work).[14] Attempts to describe other cultures, which may have no bearing on the facts of the case, can seriously affect the outcome.

In the context of the dominant culture, black women may be seen as over-protective of children, over-religious or over-punitive towards their children. This may lead to a black woman being regarded as not a 'good' mother or a 'good enough' one. Expressions of emotion like anger or affection may be misinterpreted. Value judgements made about sexual or family relationships, work status and parental responsibility, based on a Euro-centric view of society may be used to deprive an individual of her liberty. Such observations are in line with a widespread feeling amongst members of the black community that,

---

[13] *Introduction to the Probation Service*, Osler A, Waterside Press, 1995.
[14] 'Race Bias in Social Enquiry Reports', Whitehouse P, *Probation Journal*, 1983, 30: 43-49.

whatever the initiatives and 'good practice' a significant number of probation officers and social workers are racist in the assumptions they make about black families. An example of an extract from an SIR quoted by Whitehouse highlights this:

> Admittedly there is about him a mild paranoid attitude associated with his ethnic propensities. As far as I am able to ascertain, his personality is that of a normally developed person considering his background and origins.

One would hope that the modern-day monitoring process and the various checks and balances which are in place would prevent such a patently obvious statement in a PSR nowadays. But many black people stand to be convinced that the sentiment behind it has disappeared also.

Merseyside Probation Service has produced a resource pack for managing and developing anti-racist practice. It maintains that service delivery in a racist society is essentially different for black clients, and that the unequal power dynamics in the relationship between supervisor and offender in terms of colour, gender and class must be recognised.[15] McQuillan emphasises the need to acknowledge the issue of white authority and to ensure the careful construction of proposals in PSRs to be no more intrusive than is justified by the seriousness of the offence.[16] The powerful use of discriminatory language, racist stereotypes and images should be continually monitored and challenged particularly in respect of black women who face the double oppression of race and gender. Thus:

> Race does not simply make the experience of women's subordination greater, it qualitatively changes the nature of that subordination.[17]

Denny demonstrates how conventions used by probation officers in interviews, written reports and records can be discriminatory towards black offenders. The imposition of a white, Anglicised view of the nuclear family leads to inappropriate judgements about black family life: white women offenders tend to be presented under considerable stress, often due to factors beyond their control, whilst black women are frequently described as impoverished, nervous and

---

[15] *Managing and Developing Anti-Racists Practice Within Probation*, Kett J, Collett S *et al*, Merseyside Probation Research and Information Unit, 1992.

[16] *Pre-sentence Reports: An Anti-Discriminatory Perspective*, McQuillan T, Association of Black Probation Officers, 1992.

[17] *Women, Oppression and Social Work: Issues in Anti-Discriminatory Practice*, Langan M and Day L (Eds.), Routledge, 1992.

taciturn. The perception of probation officers, as well as the courts, contributes to the 'composite picture' of the way black women are perceived and sentenced.[18]

Other studies have looked more closely at the depiction of black and white defendants as offenders. This is important as the emphasis of probation work has shifted from presenting comprehensive accounts of offenders' background, personality and home circumstances to concentrating on offence seriousness, attitudes to offending and compliance with previous sentences and the risk of re-offending.[19] Waters classifies reports according to whether the defendant's race was marginal as a theme in explaining the offending; whether the defendant was depicted in terms of culture conflict; or as being 'alien' in the sense of very much 'other' to the report writer.[20] Pinder looked at explanations of offending offered in reports finding explanations focusing on opposition stances in black defendants and inadequacy in white defendants.[21] Hudson's 1988 study of reports, already mentioned, found black offenders being viewed as hostile and aggressive, and not being credited with the same attempts to change to non-criminal lifestyles that were put forward in the case of white defendants.

Crolley analysed how women offenders were portrayed in PSRs, this differing according to the gender of the author, finding little evidence by either men or women authors of stereotyping women as good mothers, wives etc., but that women officers were less likely to have their proposals followed than male officers.[22] It was suggested that the content of PSRs on women might be influenced as much by the politics of gender as a description of the offence and the offender, for example:

> There is some evidence that men authors tend to describe women offenders as being *depressed* whilst women authors describe women offenders as being *oppressed*.[23]

---

[18] *Racism and Anti-Racism in Probation*, Denney D, Routledge, 1992.

[19] In *Racism and Criminology: Concepts and Controversies in Racism and Criminology*, Hudson B (Eds. Hudson B and Cook D), Sage, 1992.

[20] 'Race and the Criminal Justice Process', Waters R, *British Journal of Criminology*, 1988, 28:82-94.

[21] 'Probation Work in a Multi-Racial Society', Pinder R, University of Leeds Applied Anthropology Group, 1984.

[22] Cited in 'A Better Service for Women', Edmunds M F, MA dissertation, unpublished, University of Exeter, 1994.

[23] Ibid.

One reason which may be contributing to some black women not receiving probation orders may be the fact that probation officers—like other criminal justice professionals—are less likely to see black offenders in problem or help terms but more in simple crime and punishment terms.[24] When probation officers are suggesting probation for black offenders, this is couched in 'nothing else has worked so we might as well try this' terms, and in terms of being able to place strictures and constraints on offenders' lives, in contrast to the positive reasons given in relation to white offenders, where the plan before the court is often posed in terms of supporting the individual in their own efforts to change. Circumstances such as unemployment and lack of housing were more often attributed to the subject's own shortcomings or personality defects when the defendant was black, rather than being discussed in relation to the difficulties caused by relationships, finances, and so on. Although women tend to be visited at home when reports are being prepared, it would appear that when it comes to black women they tend not to be because of the stereotype view of black people—again as aggressive or violent.

Note
Some further relevant information about PSRs in relation to sentencing is contained in *Chapter 5* in relation to Roger Hood's study of sentencing in the Crown Court described there.

INTERVIEWS

The women in the sample were interviewed about their experiences with the probation service and asked to give their views of their dealings with probation officers, including prison probation officers. Some of the women felt that the probation service had the potential to help black women, not only to obtain a non-custodial sentence but also with financial assistance. However, some of them considered that certain probation officers had stereotyping views of black women, and that even good PSRs written on black women were not believed in court.

Eight of the women appeared to be content with their probation officer, and with the help they had received. The officer's race did not seem to matter. Ten of the women had white probation officers and felt

---

[24] 'Penal Policy and Racial Justice', Hudson B, in Minority Ethnic Groups in the Criminal Justice System, Gelsthorp L (Ed.), Cambridge University Institute of Criminology, Cropwood Conference Series, No. 21, 1993.

that the officer had done his or her best to help them. Some felt that if represented by a black probation officer *in court* the judge might not take the PSR seriously, especially if it was a very good one, 'written on their behalf' (something which mirrors the views the women had about black lawyers: see *Chapter 5*). Whatever the colour of the probation officer's skin, the women felt the PSR would not override or influence the judge's perception of them:

> My report was good, but I felt that the judge did not take notice of it. The reason why I committed the crime was not given. (Margaret)

It is interesting that this particular woman felt that her probation officer was 'good'. A probation order had been suggested in the PSR. Her barrister was said to be 'no good' as he did not mention the reason why she committed the crime—a mitigating factor. Similarly:

> The report written for the court was O.K., but I felt that she (the probation officer) should have asked for a long term of probation . . . I wouldn't have got prison. She is good . . . she always has time to talk to me and listens. (Dawn)

One woman said that the court rejected her PSR because it was over effusive:

> My report was very good and the judge did not believe it. He felt that it was *too* good. (emphasis supplied) (Nora)

This may be because the judge had a stereotype view of the kind of a life a black woman is supposed to live. The probation officer had written about Nora's good character, and that she was a fine mother who cared for her children well—which goes against the mental picture that many white people have of the black woman.

One of the women, who got on well with her probation officer, felt that she had let him down by committing further offences:

> David (a white man) is my present probation officer. I have had a few probation officers in the past, but find I can speak to David about anything. I have been arrested a few times but have not told him because I feel I have let him down. (Sarah)

It would appear from this comment that the relationship between an offender and a probation officer, if it *is* good, can have an impact on trying to stay 'clean', or can simply make a black woman evasive.

57

The other 12 women were dissatisfied with the help they got from the probation service. Josephine said that:

> I get the impression that probation officers are not concerned about you. They see you and just keep a record.

Some of them felt that probation officers patronised them and did not try to understand 'where they were coming from'. But nonetheless some of the women had good words to say about their *prison* probation officers (i.e. those seconded to work inside a prison under the auspices of the prison governor). Probation officers who helped the women to bring their children or babies into prison were praised and described as excellent:

> When I was sent to prison my baby was three months old at the time. I wrote to my probation officer saying can you help me have my child in prison. She wrote back to say that she did not have time to come as it was too far . . . It was the probation officer in prison who helped me bring my child into prison. (Valerie)

Another woman who had received practical help from a probation officer in prison said:

> He is excellent. He really helped me. (Anna)

Four of the women felt that if the probation officer had shown more interest it would have helped them to get a lighter sentence. They believed that if probation officers had inquired more about their backgrounds they would have written more persuasive PSRs (normally only prepared before the case comes to court if the offender intends to plead guilty, and thus not usually available where a plea of 'not guilty' is entered and a trial takes place, unless and until there is a conviction and the case has afterwards been adjourned for the PSR to be prepared: except in experimental areas where special schemes operate to prepare reports ahead in all cases). Many black people plead 'not guilty': see *Chapter 5*.

One woman was dissatisfied with the probation service and felt that 'they should update their reports regularly' (something which should happen in appropriate circumstances under National Standards):

> The probation service has helped me in the past but I find they use old reports. I feel they should update them . . . sometimes I don't feel like

talking to probation officers . . . Its not their business and . . . I don't say much to them. (Edith)

Catherine, now 23 years old, had been in trouble with the law from the age of 14 and in prison before, but at the time of the interview she was on probation. She talked about her experiences:

I abused the probation service because I felt they did not care about me . . . and they did not show any interest — they did not want to get down to the real problems. So I just used them to get money for cigarettes etc. . . . I feel that it helps to have a black probation officer — that is if she is not a coconut . . . then there is no difference. I now have a black probation officer. We have a very good rapport and I feel that the fact that she is black has helped . . . as she knows where I am coming from.

It appeared that the colour of the probation officer's skin did not matter as long as he or she 'delivered the goods'. It was also clear that if the probation officer was black he or she needed to be able to understand black people and their problems, in other words they needed to remain black—hence the word coconut meaning 'black on the outside and white inside'. Great resentment was directed towards black professionals generally who did not behave as 'black'. On this question of 'coconuts' another woman said:

I felt that my probation officer was very white-minded and was asking me questions I would not expect from a black person. (Veronica)

Measures to deal with racism in probation reports have met with criticism from some judges. One circuit judge described the equal opportunities policies of the probation service, whereby reports were vetted for racial and other bias, as sinister. He claimed that:

In 30 years at the bar and four and a half years on the bench, I have never seen a probation report which contained any remark I could describe as racist, sexist or stereotyping.[25]

Although some of the women felt that their probation officer had not been helpful and could have done more it was clear from the interviews that the PSR was seen as *able* to help in reducing the sentence and that a 'caring' probation officer who advised and listened

---

[25] *The Times*, 13 September 1990.

to problems and assisted in practical ways was appreciated and deemed to be 'good'. Annette said:

> The probation officer was no good and I feel she helped me get 3 year prison sentence.

Conversely, according to Jane:

> I did not see my probation officer until the hearing day. She was not sympathetic.

Judith, a foreign woman, who did not have a PSR prepared on her felt that if she had had one it would have made a difference to the sentence she received. She had been living in the United Kingdom for six years at the time of her arrest. She was a single mother with four children and unemployed at the time of her sentence. The children were back home in the West Indies. Judith said:

> My children were suffering back home . . . and I had no money . . . I couldn't get a job and was not working. My brother-in-law took advantage of my financial situation when I went home to see my children. He said you won't be in trouble and we will give you money enough for your children fees. He said think about what the money can do to help you and your children . . . I took a chance . . . Here I am with a seven year sentence and do not know where my children are.

Geraldine, who is 'black British' (i.e. born in Britain) also did not have a PSR. She felt that one would have made a difference to the sentence she received. She was sentenced to six years imprisonment for smuggling six ounces of cocaine:

> I was finding it difficult to get a job here and decided to go abroad and work for a year. I got mixed up with the wrong crowd. I was a tour guide and also did child-minding on the side. I was doing child-minding when I was told to stay with these people at the hotel. They forced me to carry their luggage . . . I did not want to because I was suspicious. They beat me up when I refused and threatened my life. When I got to Gatwick I had a black eye and a broken tooth . . . also one tooth had fallen out. A probation report would have helped . . . I have been in prison two years now and only saw a probation officer last week.

COMMENT

A great many steps *have* been taken to remove bias in PSRs, but there is still a way to go. In many probation areas, reports now have to go through a process of quality control which is part of the wider 'equal opportunities' policy. The aim is to ensure that they are not discriminatory in their content or suggestions. It means that the probation service has adapted its practice to take account of the presence of black people in society generally and, in particular, in the offender population. Race awareness and anti-racist training courses have been provided to staff in the hope of increasing their sensitivity to black issues. However, despite widespread monitoring, gate-keeping, anti-racist training and the use of various methods to regulate decision-making, the proportion of black prisoners continues to rise and the rate of participation of black offenders in community programmes does not seem to be increasing significantly.

It could be said that some but by no means all black women face racism, sexism and classism in relation to the work of the probation service. They are sometimes considered difficult clients who are not viewed as able to change their behaviour. If black women are to fully benefit from the probation service, work needs to be done to develop further and stronger anti-racist, anti-sexist and anti-classist policies and practice in order to deliver appropriate and effective services to them.

Chapter 5

Experience of Courts and Lawyers

Despite their central position in the criminal justice process and preoccupation with fairness and impartiality, the criminal courts are not above discrimination or making misleading racist assumptions. The make up of judicial institutions raises questions about the context in which cases involving women who do not fit white male preconceptions about appropriate behaviour are heard. Similarly, sentencing and allied decision-making patterns (concerning, for example, grants of bail or requests for PSRs) raise questions whether women are treated differently to men. When information about court decision-making in relation to black people and women is viewed collectively this gives added cause for concern that disadvantage is compounded in the way described in *Chapter 1*. Details of the disproportionate number of black women who end up in prison is dealt with in *Chapter 7*.

INITIATIVES AND COURT PERSONNEL

Particularly since section 95 Criminal Justice Act 1991 (see *Chapter 1*) there has been an increasing awareness of the discrimination issues among court practitioners.

Initiatives
The Lord Chancellor's Department and Home Office have issued guidance to courts, the effect of which is to require them to develop policies and practices to ensure equality of treatment for people of all races. The Judicial Studies Board has established an Ethnic Minorities Advisory Committee and, since this was set up in 1991, training on race issues has been provided for Crown Court judges, recorders, assistant recorders and stipendiary magistrates. The Board has also held seminars on race issues for lay magistrates' training officers (who in turn make arrangements for the training of the 30,374 lay magistrates). Magistrates' training advisors have taken steps to promote good practice and consistency in training and on race issues. The Court Service (responsible for all but magistrates' courts) has carried out pilot training courses in conjunction with NACRO's Race Unit for court ushers and administrative staff: this has been taken up

63

nationally by the Lord Chancellor's Department as a model of good practice. Following a review of equal opportunities in the Court Service, the Service has relaunched its equal opportunities policy, together with an equal opportunities helpline.

Independently, the Justices' Clerks' Society has published two wide ranging documents, 'Dealing with Disadvantage' (1990) and 'Black People in Magistrates' Courts' (1995), which contain detailed information and recommendations to promote equality and avoid discrimination.

Court personnel

There are no High Court judges from minority ethnic groups. In 1995, just five of the 514 circuit judges, two of the 339 district judges, 13 of the 897 recorders and nine of the 341 assistant recorders were from minority ethnic groups. In 1995, 1.3 per cent of judicial appointments were from minority ethnic groups compared with 0.87 per cent in 1992. In June 1995, 4 per cent of solicitors and 6 per cent of barristers were from minority ethnic groups, compared to 1.3 per cent and 4 per cent respectively in 1989.[1]

At the time of writing (April, 1997), there are no current figures for the number of black magistrates or magistrates from minority ethnic groups. In 1989, the proportion was just under 2 per cent. However, 9.1 per cent of all newly appointed magistrates in 1996 (110 out of 1,682) were from minority ethnic groups compared with 4.7 per cent in 1989 and 8.1 per cent in 1995. Of the 110 magistrates appointed from minority ethnic groups in 1996, 44 were women and 66 men.[2] In 1997, there were no black justices' clerks. In 1995, 17 of the 370 deputy clerks and 21 of the 1,470 court ushers were from minority groups.[3]

BACKGROUND

Historically in Britain the law, including the criminal law, has been made or determined largely by white males and, as has already been indicated above, the great majority of people in senior positions in judicial institutions are white men. The basis of knowledge of

---

[1] 'Race, Discrimination and the Criminal Justice System', NAPO and ABPO, August 1996.

[2] The 1996 figures were published in *The Magistrate*, April 1997.

[3] 'Race, Discrimination and the Criminal Justice System', NAPO and ABPO, August 1996. Updated to 1997 for justices' clerks.

legislators and judges is thus located in whatever institutionalised discrimination may exist. Such comments cannot be applied in their full rigour to the lay magistracy which, as of 1996, was made up of 15,858 men and 14,516 women with 9.1 per cent of the total from minority ethnic groups (see above).

Apart from setting out criminal offences, the law, in effect, defines acceptable behaviour, for example affecting marriage, sexual relations, domestic violence and the care of children, and sets the parameters of what is 'normal' or 'proper'. This 'man-made' law sets the context within which courts respond to women, and to particular groups such as black women, mothers, victims of domestic violence, prostitutes and lesbians. Judges and magistrates—many of whom are middle-class white men—then administer the law in the light of their own perceptions of black women. Notoriously, Lord Denning, in the original version of his book, *What's Next in the Law?* stated:

> . . . There are white and black, coloured and brown . . . some of them come from countries where bribery and graft are accepted . . . where stealing is a virtue so long as you are not found out.[4]

Although he was questioning the fitness of black people to serve as jurors, this type of sentiment may indicate how some judges and possibly magistrates think of foreign defendants. The book was withdrawn and amended.

The tendency to categorise women who do not match the expectations of the dominant culture as possessing criminal potential has been noted in *Chapter 2*. Despite positive changes and the recognition of the existence of equal rights, deep-rooted problems of institutional inequality persist and the administration of the law continues to reflect this: the political, social and economic dominance of white people and to a large extent white men. Their beliefs about the role of women in the home and at work reinforce popular attitudes about women. Kennedy maintains that the law mirrors society and continues to reflect the subordination of women.[5] Similarly, the construction of defendants as white and British (or perhaps nowadays European) reinforces and perpetuates racism.

There has been no direct focus on black women's experience of sentencing practice. There are, however, certain clues which suggest that there is a need for concern. Because *women* appear before the courts less frequently than men they may be seen as out of place, not as

---

[4] *What's Next in the Law?*, Lord Denning, Butterworths, 1982.
[5] *Eve Was Framed*, Kennedy H, Chatto and Windus, 1992.

'offenders' in the way that men are. But this general perception does not seem to apply to *black women,* when it may not be considered at all unusual for them to be involved in criminal activity. Women who appear 'unusual' or 'abnormal' because of their behaviour or lifestyle may be sentenced in a different way to those who conform to a more traditional role.[6] Judges and magistrates, whatever their declared intent, may react negatively to women whose dress or hair is unconventional. This also applies to women whose sexuality or racial origins appear to challenge the court,[7] and it seems obvious that a defendant's demeanour can have an effect on whether a court, for example, believes a claim of future good intentions or remorse, either of which may affect the outcome. Hedderman suggests that women may receive more lenient sentences than men.[8] However, the repercussions for women who do not subscribe to anticipated behaviour can be quite the opposite, and this would include black women. Being married, for example, has been found to mitigate more strongly against detention for black women in the USA.[9] As pointed out in earlier chapters, stereotyping and cultural assumptions based on the fact that black women may not act 'normally' can be highly misleading as indicators of criminal behaviour.

COURT DECISION-MAKING

In addition to the paucity of information which exists about the sentencing of black women *per se,* until recently it has not been possible to isolate the effect of race in sentencing and to separate this from decisions made at other points in the criminal justice process. Similarly, research studies tended in the main to be inconclusive about unequal treatment of white defendants and black defendants.

Roger Hood's Study
In 1992, the most thorough and academically rigorous research study ever carried out in Britain was published. Dr. Roger Hood, Director of the Centre for Criminological Research at Oxford University, examined sentences passed in 3,317 cases heard at a number of Crown Court

---

[6] 'Women on Trial: A Study of the Female Defendant', Edwards S, Manchester University Press, 1984; 'The Effect of Defendants' Demeanour on Sentencing in Magistrates' Courts', Hedderman C, *Home Office Research Bulletin No. 29,* 1990.

[7] *Paying for Crime,* Carlen P and Cook D, Open University Press, 1989.

[8] Hedderman C, 1990: see footnote 6.

[9] 'Structures and Practice of Familial-Based Justice in a Criminal Court', Daly K, *Law and Society Review,* 1987, 21:2.

centres in the West Midlands during 1989.[10] This showed that, overall, black males were 17 per cent more likely to receive a custodial sentence than their white counterparts. Even after controlling for 15 key variables relating to the seriousness of the offence and other legally relevant factors, the study disclosed that black people had a greater chance of going to prison, to the extent of between five and eight per cent. In cases of medium gravity—where a judge's discretion was, seemingly, the greatest—this rose to 13 per cent. The study concluded that:

> Eighty per cent of the over-representation of black men in the prison population was due to the disproportionate number of them appearing before the Crown Courts (reflecting of course decisions made at all previous stages of the criminal justice process) and the seriousness of their cases. The remaining 20 per cent . . . could only be explained as a result of differential treatment by the courts and other factors influencing the severity of the sentences they received. One third of this 'race effect' was due to the higher proportion pleading not guilty and the longer prison terms they got as a result . . . It would not need many courts to behave as the Dudley courts and the courts at Warwick and Stafford appear to have done for it to have a considerable effect on the racial composition of the prison population.

The study also found that significantly higher proportions of black (42 per cent) and Asian (43 per cent) offenders were sentenced without a pre-sentence report (PSR: then called a 'social inquiry report, or 'SIR'). This compared with 28 per cent for white offenders. This was in part due to the fact that more black and Asian defendants pleaded 'not guilty' and the existing practice not to prepare such reports in advance unless there was a guilty plea, or following conviction after an adjournment for this purpose, which the judge was not always prepared to allow. There were also significant racial disparities in the distribution of community sentences. For a general discussion of PSRs and their relationship to community sentences see *Chapter 4*.

After taking account of factors influencing the severity of a sentence, it was found that black adults were given sentences higher up the tariff than white people. Concentrated largely within the 'medium risk of custody' band, black defendants were:

- more likely to receive a custodial sentence;
- less likely to be given community service or a probation order;

---

[10] *Race and Sentencing: A Study in the Crown Court*, Clarendon Press, 1992; *A Question of Judgement: Summary of 'Race and Sentencing'*, Commission for Racial Equality, 1993.

- less likely to be recommended for probation; and
- even when recommended for probation, less likely to get it.

Among young offenders with offences falling within this band, black offenders were more likely to get community service or be sent to an attendance centre and less likely to be placed on probation. The study concluded that:

> The evidence supports the contention that black offenders receive sentences which are higher up the 'tariff' of penalties than do whites and, therefore, put at more risk of getting a prison sentence should they re-appear on fresh charges.

As if to corroborate this, Home Office Statistical Bulletin 21/94, which among other things examined differences in types of offence, type of court and number of previous convictions, these and certain other factors affect the overall position: more black offenders were serving sentences for drugs offences for which sentences are frequently lengthy, more black offenders are sentenced at the Crown Court where sentences tend to be more severe for similar offences— 'But significant differences remain in sentence lengths for unlawful wounding, theft, handling stolen property, drugs offences and some others.'[11]

Figures contained in 'The Ethnic Origins of Prisoners' (*Home Office Statistical Bulletin*, 1994) showed that 39 per cent of white males aged under 21 received into prison had six or more previous convictions compared with 27 per cent of young blacks and 18 per cent of young Asian prisoners. The figures for males aged 21 and over were 60 per cent, 48 per cent and 28 per cent respectively. Black prisoners were serving longer sentences: in mid-1994, 58 per cent of black sentenced adult males were serving sentences of over four years, compared with 41 per cent of white males. The study examined how far differences in sentence lengths could be explained by differences in types of offence (e.g. more black offenders were serving sentences for drugs offences for which sentences are frequently lengthy); the type of court at which sentence was passed (a greater proportion of black offenders are sentenced at the Crown Court, where sentences tend to be more severe than at magistrates' courts for comparable offences); and by the number of previous convictions.

A study of the sentencing of juveniles in Wolverhampton[12] found that African-Caribbean defendants had significantly more high tariff

---

[11] 'Race and Criminal Justice', Penal Affairs Consortium, September 1996, p.5.

[12] *Negative Images*, Kirk, B, Avebury, 1996.

non-custodial sentences (particularly supervision orders with requirements and community service orders) than white or Asian defendants—a distinction which cannot be explained by differences in the seriousness of offences, and which occurred although African-Caribbean defendants had, on average, committed fewer current offences and had shorter existing criminal records.

The data in Hood's study analysed PSRs and showed that these were more likely to propose high tariff sentences on African-Caribbean defendants in circumstances where such proposals would not have been made if the defendant had been white. While, in general, PSRs described African-Caribbean defendants in a positive or balanced way, report writers, for well-intentioned reasons, also included background information on defendants, which was in practice likely to reinforce stereotypical views of black families and lead to more substantial intervention in the form of a high tariff sentence.

In 1993, a paper prepared for the Royal Commission on Criminal Procedure by Marian Fitzgerald, reviewed the key findings from research. She concluded:

> The research available addresses many of the concerns which have been raised by ethnic minorities about their experience of criminal justice. It does not do so definitely, however, and many gaps remain. Yet Hood adds weight to the evidence already accumulated which strongly suggests that, even where differences in social and legal factors are taken into account, there are ethnic differences in outcomes which can only be explained in terms of discrimination.

The first publication on race as a result of section 95 Criminal Justice Act 1991 was the Home Office booklet *Race and Criminal Justice* (1992), which pointed out that:

> At present there is only limited information available on any part of this subject. Research findings to date have been patchy in their coverage. Both statistics and research findings, however, provide evidence which support the concerns which have been expressed about differential treatment of Afro-Caribbean (that is, people of West Indian or African origin) . . .

> Afro-Caribbeans are significantly more likely than whites to be stopped by the police even when other relevant factors such as age and employment are taken into account . . . Afro-Caribbeans are more likely than whites to be remanded in custody before trial . . . The type of offence with which they are charged only partly explains this difference; and a higher

proportion of Afro-Caribbeans who have spent time in custody on remand are subsequently acquitted . . .

Afro-Caribbeans are more likely than whites to be tried at the Crown Court. This partly because they are more likely to be charged with indictable-only offences. They are also more likely to be tried at the Crown Court in triable-either-way cases. Afro-Caribbean defendants themselves are more likely to elect Crown Court trial. Local studies in Leeds have shown that magistrates are also more likely to have declined jurisdiction in such cases.

Bail and remand
Hood's study disclosed that a higher proportion of black people (26 per cent) than white people (20 per cent) had been refused bail. It was estimated by him that there was a 16 per cent greater likelihood of black offenders ending up in custody on remand after taking into account all available relevant factors. Another study by Imogen Brown and Roy Hullin[13] of contested bail applications coming before Leeds magistrates' court during a six months period in 1989 found no difference between the proportion of white and African-Caribbean defendants who were remanded in custody when the prosecution opposed bail. However, there *was* evidence to suggest that the Crown Prosecution Service opposed bail in a higher proportion of cases involving black defendants than white defendants. The authors commented:

> . . . if a larger proportion of ethnic minority defendants make bail applications which are opposed, and are thereafter remanded in custody by magistrates in the same proportion as white defendants, there will be an imbalance in the overall remand picture.

A higher proportion of sentenced black prisoners were refused bail before trial. The data suggests that part of the difference in treatment between ethnic groups may be accounted for by the type and seriousness of the offence (as measured by the sentence length). However, after allowing for this, statistically significant differences still remained for adult males convicted of wounding (where 59 per cent of black prisoners had been refused bail compared with 43 per cent of white prisoners); fraud and forgery (55 per cent compared with 40 per cent); drug offences (74 per cent compared with 56 per cent); and some other offences.

---

[13] 'Contested Bail Applications: The Treatment of Ethnic Minority and White Offenders', *Criminal Law Review*, 1993, 107.

WOMEN AND THE COURTS

Black women's specific experiences have again lacked specific attention. But, as intimated in *Chapter 1*, there *is* evidence that women in general receive unequal treatment compared with men at various stages of the criminal justice process. As indicated in *Chapter 4*, foreign women often do not benefit from having a PSR which may mitigate the effect of their sentence (even though the PSR is not designed for this purpose). Their home or family circumstances are thus not always taken into account. Many African women in prison are there for their first offence and have no previous criminal record. The disproportionate number of black women in prison is discussed in *Chapter 7*. Certain key points can be made here about the court stage of this process.

In 1994, eight per cent of adult women sentenced for indictable offences received prison sentences compared with six per cent in 1992. Twenty per cent of adult men received prison sentences in 1994, reflecting that, on average, sentenced male offenders are convicted of more serious offences and have more previous convictions than women offenders.

A lower proportion of women offenders are fined (28 per cent compared with 36 per cent) or given community service orders (7 per cent compared with 11 per cent), whereas more are given probation orders (19 per cent compared with 11 per cent).

It has been observed by several commentators that when the defendant is black, offences are more likely to be described in such a way that they come into a more serious category. Crow and Cove found that when black people were charged with assault there were more cases where the 'victim' had suffered no actual injury than when the defendants were white.[14] There must, presumably, have been scope for reduction of the charges or for non-prosecution. This accords with the evidence from the USA where studies have found that charges against black assailants, especially if the victims are white, are less likely to be downgraded than in the case of white defendants.[15] It has been observed that white victims' sufferings are more likely to be seen as serious, and therefore the assailants deserving of more serious

---

[14] 'Ethnic Minorities in the Courts', Crow I and Cove J, Criminal Law Review, 1984, 413-417.

[15] 'Race and Prosecution Discretion in Homicide Cases', Radelet M and Pierce G, *Law and Society Review*, 1985, 19,4: 587-621.

punishment than black victims' assailants.[16] So black on white crime is likely to be sentenced more severely than either white on black or black on black, again suggesting that race is a factor in criminal justice decision-making including sentencing.

Legal variables, such as offence type and previous criminal history are not the only ones which affect sentencing. Unemployment and no permanent address, family or other community ties, have also been shown to correlate with sentences given by magistrates' courts and Crown Courts. Unemployment in borderline cases may be the deciding factor as to whether someone is sent to prison.

As indicated in *Chapter 4*, there is also room for concern that women convicted of minor offences are more likely to receive probation orders in circumstances where men are fined, making it less likely that courts will regard a further probation order or other community sentence appropriate if they reoffend and moving them more quickly up the tariff of non-custodial sentences towards custody. There is also evidence indicating that some imprisoned women may have been regarded wrongly as less suitable for community service orders or intensive probation programmes than male offenders in similar circumstances.[17]

It is instructive to consider the profile of women who receive prison sentences. According to the Penal Affairs Consortium:

Most women prisoners were living in poverty before going to prison, often facing multiple debts. The process of imprisonment frequently results in loss of accommodation and possessions and increased destitution on release, pushing them into a downward spiral of hardship . . . Many women prisoners are the mothers of young children who have to be looked after by makeshift arrangements involving relatives or taken into care. Such separations can have a traumatic effect on young children, can adversely affect their long term intellectual and emotional development, and may be a cause of later delinquency or instability. This means that policies supposedly intended to combat crime are increasingly likely to be a cause of crime in future generations . . . The Penal Affairs Consortium considers that the trend towards a greater use of imprisonment for women is a mistaken one which will cause more damage to society than it prevents.[18]

---

[16] 'Making the Punishment Fit the Crime', Zimring F E, Hastings Centre, Report No. 6, 1976.

[17] See 'Women Offenders and Probation Service Provision', Home Office, 1991: 'Provision for Women', Marie Edmonds, Somerset Probation Service, November, 1993.

[18] 'The Imprisonment of Women: Some Facts and Figures', Penal Affairs Consortium, March 1996.

Women and bail

Before conviction or sentence, black women may be remanded in custody for reasons of perceived offence seriousness linked to race, failure to satisfy what in the case of white people might be bail conditions, or to make themselves available for, or cooperate in the preparation of, PSRs. Groups such as NACRO, the Howard League for Penal Reform and the Prison Reform Trust have expressed concern about the disproportionate number of women (compared to men) who are denied bail and who subsequently receive a non-custodial sentence.[19] The Howard League estimated that in 1990 only 23 per cent of women who had spent time in custody on remand were subsequently received into prison under sentence, and that up to 73 per cent of women spending time in custody on remand were there unnecessarily.[20] The difficulties encountered by defendants who are remanded into custody (such as loss of accommodation, separation from relatives and family, lack of contact with a defence lawyer and poor physical and sanitary conditions) are likely to be experienced more acutely by women than men. The limited number of female prison places means that, taking this group as a whole, women are held further away from their home area. NACRO maintains that women in custody on remand effectively serve a prison sentence, often in the most overcrowded parts of the penal system, even if subsequently found not guilty or given a non-custodial sentence. This experience, which may also result in the loss of employment, accommodation, family and other community ties, can increase the risk of offending.

The National Association of Probation Officers (NAPO) considered that women may be remanded in custody because of the limited number of bail hostel places.[21] Many women could, however, be remanded to addresses in their local community. Equally, many women are remanded for medical reports but later receive non-custodial sentences.[22] Schemes to provide access to an adequate number of bail hostel places, bail support programmes for women, and associated bail information provision need to be looked at with a view to their being provided in each court area.

---

[19] *The Guardian*, 25 March 1994.

[20] Crook F in *Discrimination in the Criminal Justice System in Values, Gender and Offending*, Senior P and Williams B (Eds.), Pavic, 1993.

[21] 'Women in Custody', NAPO, May 1989.

[22] 'Sex, Class and Crime: Towards a Non-Sexist Criminology', Gregory J, in *Confronting Crime, Mathhews* , R and Young J (Eds.), Sage, 1986. pp. 53-71.

Black women are more frequently refused bail, and this may partly be because of not having what is perceived as a stable family background. There appears to be a general assumption that ethnic minority women will 'disappear into their own subculture' which it will then be difficult for the police to penetrate. In addition poverty within the black community often means that it is difficult to obtain financial sureties or a security (the latter, though relatively rarely used for black people or white people, involves the deposit of a sum of money or other valuables with the court). Such considerations mean that black women who should be on bail may often find it being refused.

This view is supported by Voakes and Fowler who maintain 'that more black people find themselves in prison than whites who have committed the same type of offences, and who are likely to have worse criminal records.'[23] Similarly, Smith[24] urges that 'African-Caribbeans may tend to be remanded in custody rather than bailed because their family circumstances tend not to meet criteria commonly used in making decisions about awarding bail.' Smith concludes that this might affect conviction rates probably because it is more difficult to prepare a defence in custody. It is also a possibility that some people remanded in custody are more likely to receive a custodial sentence, almost as if the very existence of such a remand predicted or justified this course. He suggests that recognition of the African-Caribbean family patterns and traditions as normal could ease the difficulty black people have in obtaining bail and notes the ways in which the laws of England and Wales traditionally 'express national identity' by excluding or marginalising present-day ethnic minorities.

Some black women defendants in criminal cases are at a particular disadvantage because they do not reside in this country and therefore have difficulty getting bail, the authorities fearing that they may fail to surrender at the end of the bail period. Because of the absence of local family ties or local connections, some of them have no one to stand surety (i.e. to vouch for their reappearance at court or at a police station).

The Runnymede Trust in its research report, 'White Justice', found that more black people were denied bail compared to their white counterparts. There are various discretionary reasons why someone can be refused bail pursuant to the Bail Act 1976. The police have to decide whether to release an individual from custody until he or she is

---

[23] 'Sentencing, Race and Social Enquiry Reports', Voakes R and Fowler Q, West Yorkshire Probation Service, 1989.

[24] 'Race, Crime and Criminal Justice', Smith D, in *Oxford Handbook of Criminology*, Maguire M and Reiner R (Eds.), Oxford University Press, 1994.

due to attend court or whether to keep him or her in police custody until his or her appearance before a magistrates' court. In the case of 'police bail' (i.e. bail granted by the police as opposed to a court) this will be for someone to return to a police station at a later date even though they have not been charged with any criminal offence.

Under the 1976 Act, the main exceptions to the right to bail are that there are substantial grounds for believing that, if granted bail, an accused person will:

- fail to surrender to bail; or
- commit an offence; or
- interfere with witnesses or otherwise obstruct the course of justice.

Bail can also be refused for the accused person's own protection. Reasons must be given by magistrates' courts to support a refusal of bail or to support conditions attached to a grant of bail.

The facts relied on when operating the Bail Act may be indirectly discriminatory, the sort of items which may have racially disadvantageous connotations. These include: a home with, say, a spouse or parent; a long-standing tenancy or other residential arrangements; a job, or at least reasonable prospects of employment; community ties to groups or associates which are regarded as 'respectable'. These are the very advantages black people have the greatest difficulty in obtaining, and yet they are the very things which often underpin the application of the statutory criteria for remand decisions.

LAWYERS

In June 1995, four per cent of solicitors and eight per cent of barristers were from ethnic minority groups, compared with 1.3 per cent and four per cent respectively in 1989. So far as the Crown Prosecution Service (CPS) is concerned, in 1995 four of the staff in higher grades (grades 1 to 6) (1.6 per cent), 90 of that service's 1,255 legal assistants (7.1 per cent), 77 of the 1,327 executive officers (5.8 per cent) and 205 of the 2,384 administrative officers (8.6 per cent) were from minority ethnic groups. Although the proportion of all CPS staff from minority ethnic groups rose from 5.9 per cent in 1991 to 7.5 per cent in 1995, the proportion in the higher grades fell from 1.9 per cent to 1.6 per cent. [25]

---

[25] 'Race Discrimination and the Criminal Justice System', NAPO and ABPO, 1996.

As can be seen from the women's interviews later in this chapter, some black defendants experience conflict in deciding whether it is better to have a white lawyer who they believe is less likely to lose the sympathy of the court or a black lawyer who understands their own culture.

Police stations have a list of duty solicitors who, mostly speaking, provide 24 hour cover on a rota basis. These solicitors can be called upon any time of the day or night. It is possible that, in some situations, police officers contact those duty solicitors who are 'amenable' to their own police practices, and who they can work easily with, as opposed to those they see as 'working against' them. Given the existence of prejudice in the ranks of the police as described in *Chapter 3*, the outcome may be less acceptable in the case of black people than white people. Something intended to assist in a practical way becomes tainted by individual or institutionalised discrimination.

Difficulties may also be experienced by black women wanting to change their lawyers. It is, of course, difficult to know how much of the dissatisfaction disclosed in the interviews which follow was due to the solicitor being unhelpful, how much was due to disappointment with the outcomes of a case and how much to the existing mistrust between black women and the criminal justice agencies.

Helena Kennedy[26] discusses the case of a black woman who saw her solicitor on only a few brief visits and her barrister, whom she had never met before, arrived just 15 minutes before the start of the case. Her regular solicitor was away on holiday, so there was no familiar face at court. Defendants in such cases have little power, and at times feel forced to accept second-rate practices from the legal profession.

Kennedy describes another case of a black woman whose English was negligible and she too was dissatisfied with her representation because—although she had had a conference with a barrister at the prison—someone else turned up at court on the day. She could not believe that it was sufficient for someone to read the papers in the case and to talk with her for as little as half an hour. It is hardly unreasonable for clients to want the opportunity to talk to their lawyers at length if they are facing a significant risk of losing their liberty or a substantial period imprisonment. But there is often a sense of pressure from the court to get a move on, and lawyers tend to fear a judge's wrath. The incidence of such changes can only be reduced if more and more cases are given fixed dates in advance.[27]

---

[26] *Eve was Framed*, Kennedy H, Chatto and Windus, 1992.
[27] Ibid.

Kennedy's description[28] of the experiences of some black women lawyers gives room for concern that the problems of black advocates being taken seriously are exacerbated in the case of women and that the difficulty of securing authority within the courtroom are even greater. Those who *are* successful, she adds, are constantly told by white colleagues that they do not seem to be black, as though there is some special stamp of blackness which they had shrugged off. Such comments may be intended as compliments but can be deeply offensive. Kennedy mentions a black woman barrister—a rising criminal practitioner—defending a black client—who had a strong feeling that the trial judge, renowned for rudeness, was particularly dismissive of her arguments. At one stage when she sat down, he sent her a note asking whether her accent was English, and if so where she had been to school. She ignored the note, uncertain what it meant, but felt undermined, as though her fluency and education were in question. After this black lawyer's final speech to the jury, the judge summed up to the all-white jury with the words: 'Members of the jury, we are British'.

INTERVIEWS

The women in the sample talked about their experiences of the courts and about magistrates, judges, sentencing, bail and lawyers. They criticised the provision of legal aid as inadequate and, typical of their comments, believed that for them there appeared to be one justice for the poor and another for the rich.

Judges and magistrates
All the women were convinced that judges and magistrates are racist. Edith said:

> I have no faith in magistrates—I feel you are found guilty the minute they see your colour—I do not think they should go through the procedure of hearing the case when they have made up their minds the minute they saw you. (Edith)

Magistrates' courts tended to be seen as 'police courts' because, the women said, magistrates are more likely to believe the police. Such views have, seemingly, resulted in a higher proportion of black defendants choosing to be tried at Crown Court whenever they have

---

[28] Ibid.

this option with the greater likelihood of a custodial sentence if convicted.[29] Such moves may also result in longer sentences, as guilty plea discount is not applicable. Proportionately more black than white defendants may also be committed for trial at the Crown Court because of representations by the Crown prosecutor rather election for trial with a view to pleading not guilty before a jury.[30] However, this must now be viewed in the light of initiatives by the CPS to combat discrimination. The women believed that in some instances, it was arranged for 'tough' judges or magistrates to deal with their cases.

Some of the women talked of certain Crown Court judges being known for being anti-black. Doreen said:

A black person is guilty before he is even tried. There are judges who don't like blacks. You get to know certain courts you go to . . . there are particular judges. The judge in my case was . . . anti-blacks. Judges don't sympathise with anyone.

Anthea also said:

I have been in trouble with the law few times. Where I live every black person knows about this judge in the Crown Court . . . He is definitely anti-black and dishes out long sentences to blacks. You just get caught up in the system.

Judge Pickles, during an interview with *The Voice* newspaper, said that:

A Rastafarian standing in front of you with dreadlocks can look rather intimidating. If we could understand their minds better, we might be able to better understand what they are doing and why they are doing it. There is no deliberate racism but there may be unconscious bias because we don't know enough about the people.[31]

Also in 1990, another judge was reported to have referred to black people as 'nig nogs'. Such a comment illustrate the racism present at influential levels. Seemingly, unless judges are prepared to examine

---

[29] 'Sentencing Practice in the Crown Court', Moxon D, Home Office Research Study No. 103, Home Office, 1988.
[30] 'A Study of Sentencing in the Leeds Magistrates' Courts', Brown I and Hullin R, *British Journal of Criminology*, 1992, 32,1: 41-53.
[31] *The Voice*, 11 September 1990.

their behaviour and admit that discriminatory practices or racism exists within their ranks, more black people will continue to end up in prison.

Bail

Fifteen of the women complained about not being able to get bail:

> I was refused bail and they said this was because I might commit further offences . . . but this was my first offence . . . and they had my passport and clothes. (Doreen)

Marva went on to say that:

> I feel I was refused bail because of my colour. Although I am naturalised, I am still treated differently from English people . . . My co-defendant is black . . . if you are black and born here you stand a better chance compared to a foreign black woman . . . Don't get me wrong we are all discriminated against but it's worse if you are foreign.

Marva's co-defendant had been charged with the same offence and according to her this was their first time in trouble with the law. Similarly, Susan, a foreign woman, was left wondering why she was refused bail when her co-defendant had been granted it. Four of the other women expressed the same view. They all felt that black women were discriminated against and that if you are a foreign black woman, even though you had lived here for years, you will get 'worse' treatment. She felt this harsher treatment was intended to send a strong message that corruption and criminal activities by foreigners will not be tolerated in Britain. If this is the case, it may be due to unjustified assumptions and racism on the part of the judiciary which sees foreign *black* women as invading their country and coming from corrupt places as if to influence their good law-abiding women.

Two of the women felt that the courts asked for a large sum of money which they knew the women did not have, including Josephine:

> They asked for a huge sum of money and my brother's ex-wife put up surety for my brother, my brother's girlfriend and myself. They asked for £2,000. (Josephine)

The relatives would, in effect, have to satisfy the court that they could raise the £2,000 if needed.

Sentence

All the women interviewed felt aggrieved and were dissatisfied with the sentences they were given. They said that after discussing them with other women in prison they realised that white women get shorter sentences compared to black women. The following are the views of some of the women:

> I feel that the judge made up his mind the minute we walked into the court. We were only there for ten minutes. (Karen)

> Before I came to this prison we found out that a white woman who had ten kilos of cannabis was given 18 months and for the same quantity a black woman in the prison was given three years. (Monica)

> I feel that the sentence is a bit rough . . . four and a half years — too long for a first offence (robbery). One white woman here has committed seven robberies in the past few years and only got five years. (Margaret)

> I was given two and a half years. I felt it was unfair for a first offence and the barrister agreed with me at the time that the sentence was harsh. One white girl here had two ounces of heroin and was given two years and this is not fair — I had two ounces. (Lorraine)

> I'm not happy with the sentence. I tried to appeal and was turned down. I have found out that white girls here got shorter sentences compared to me — some black girls got even longer sentences than me — especially the foreign ones. (Geraldine)

This was echoed by Dawn who said:

> Courts are not fair. I had one and a half kilo of cocaine and was given ten years and have done four years so far. Since I have been in prison I have found that some white women, although they had more cocaine on them, got lesser sentences. One white woman here had six kilos and was given five years. I feel it's unfair as it is my first offence. (Dawn)

> I was given six years for six ounces of cocaine and have found that some inmates have got lesser sentences even though they had more heroin on them. One white woman had one kilo and got four years. (Cynthia)

It is difficult to say how much of this was due to legitimate considerations (such as the seriousness of the offence, the offender's past criminal record and the exact circumstances of the offence) and how much was due to extra-legal variables (being black, being a woman, belonging to the working-classes). Moreover most of the

80

women interviewed pleaded 'not guilty', thereby forfeiting any discount for guilty plea (usually up to one third: there being a statutory duty to consider this aspect).

Lawyers
An area for concern for the women interviewed was not being able to see a duty solicitor on the first day of their arrest. Twelve of the women had not been allowed to see, or had not been told about seeing, one:

> I was not told about a duty solicitor and did not see one while I was in police custody. (Geraldine)

Sixteen of the women complained about the kind of advice they got from the duty solicitor. Aisha said:

> I felt that the duty solicitor was conspiring with the police. You just couldn't trust him.

This may be partly due to the mistrust which already exists between black people and criminal justice agencies. It may not necessarily be that an individual solicitor is racist, but that, since he or she is part of the system, he or she is not seen as being fair in assessing the position of a black woman suspect or defendant, or in giving advice. Several of the women were convinced that the duty solicitor was not working in their favour but against them:

> The duty solicitor was not helpful and I eventually changed him . . . I felt he was helping the police. (Josephine)

> I feel we get solicitors who work for the system — my solicitor — I could not trust him. (Nancy)

Miriam, who wanted to change the duty solicitor but failed, said:

> He was a 'custom' solicitor. I didn't find him helpful. All he said to me was . . . tell them the truth and you will be alright. He refused to see me alone. I wanted to change him when I was on remand, but they wouldn't let me.

One woman described how she took over from her solicitor in court and represented herself:

> The solicitor I had was no good. I said I prefer to speak for myself . . . and in the end . . . I just put on a good show and was given six month's

81

probation. I would have got a prison sentence if I had let the solicitor speak for me. (Doreen)

Another said that because of the experience she had had with solicitors in the past (she had been in trouble with the law since the age of 13) she felt black people should be encouraged to represent themselves:

> . . . There is nothing you can do if you are not happy with a solicitor. You can't really defend yourself. You are not allowed to say anything. Somebody else has to speak for you or defend you . . . All they do is bring up your bad points especially when you are black. (Cora)

Aisha who had wanted to change her solicitor but failed said:

> I wanted to change my solicitor but was refused. I had a co-defendant who was trying to put all the blame on me . . . but even for this reason they refused to change him.

Two of the women did feel that duty solicitors had done their best and had told them that they were allowed to make a telephone call to their children:

> I was worried about my children and when I told the duty solicitor . . . he said 'Yes, you can make a phone call' . . . and I did. (Doreen)

All the women felt that they had been treated unfairly by the courts and ten of them that the 'longer sentences' they received were due partly to the legal advice they were given. Four of the women felt that if you are on legal aid you do not get 'justice'.

> I feel that legal aid clients do not get a fair deal. I do not feel that barristers and solicitors take your cases seriously . . . unless you are paying for yourself. (June)

Some advocates who take on legal aid clients are young, liberal and with a conviction that everybody should get justice regardless of whether they are poor or not. Hence their willingness to take legal aid cases which usually means a long delay in payment and lesser fees than for private client work. It may lead to economies:

> My barrister only saw me 15 minutes before the hearing. There is no way he would have known all about me in 15 minutes. (Doreen)

This is supported by the black women prisoner's views as detailed in my own earlier research.[32]

> I saw the barrister 20 minutes before the hearing. If he wanted to know more about me and my case he would have seen me earlier or for a longer time like an hour or so before the hearing. (Jackie)

> These solicitors and barristers are no good. They forget that the decision is very important to you. (Maxine)

This could be said to be a common complaint by defendants, particularly if convicted or given what they believe is an excessive sentence. However, two women *were* pleased, or partly so, with their lawyer's performance:

> My barrister did his best. . . at the end of the day it's not up to him. (Judith)

> My solicitor was very good and interested. My barrister was not good. I was charged with possession and supply but the barrister insisted that I should plead guilty to both charges so I could get a lighter sentence . . . I was not guilty of both charges that is why I did not want to plead guilty . . I took his advice and pleaded guilty. (Marva)

Marva felt that the barrister had advised her to plead guilty because he believed she was guilty of both charges despite explaining to him that she was not guilty of either. She felt that the advice she got from her barrister was because '. . . the barrister believed every black person is guilty' and Marva was also unhappy with the length of her sentence, which she felt was too long.

It is difficult to know what constitutes a good barrister or solicitor. To these women it did not seem to matter so much whether it was a black or white lawyer, as long as he or she turned out to be 'good'. It would appear that a 'good' advocate is measured by the interest he or she shows in the case, the advice, the time he or she spends listening and advising and also partly by the kind of sentence an offender gets. For example Cora said:

> I was convicted of fraud involving £75 at the post office. I was 17 at the time I committed the crime and the final hearing took place four years

---

[32] 'The Criminalisation and Imprisonment of Black Women', *Probation Journal*, Chigwada R, September 1989, pp. 100-105.

later. I feel I got a lighter sentence (18 months in prison) because of my good barrister.

Most of the women were aware of the problems which black lawyers face in the system. Four of the women who had been in trouble with the law several times talked about their experiences in court concerning black barristers:

> I've been in trouble with the law a few times so I know how to handle the system . . . what I do is to go and see a black solicitor first and then study my case and ask to be represented by a white barrister. I'll study my case and tell the barrister the points I want stressed. (Sarah)

Rhona said:

> I feel black lawyers are looked upon as inferior. I prefer to take my case to a black solicitor's firm because I feel at ease to talk to him about my case . . . this is from my experience anyway . . . black solicitors understand where black people are coming from. I get a white barrister to represent me in court . . . The judges and magistrates have no respect for black lawyers . . . I know this is supporting the system . . . but that verdict is very important to you . . . and sometimes you have to look after number one.

This was echoed by Doreen:

> If I can help it I would not be represented by a black barrister . . . they have to be very careful because the judge can belittle them . . . or find themselves apologising more.

Black lawyers are often said to be too close to the client and this is viewed as stopping them from giving professional and independent advice. The judges have been known to belittle black lawyers. This perception is supported by *Beatrice's Case* (see *Chapter 6*), where the judge did not seem to have much patience with Beatrice's co-accused's black barrister. (Beatrice herself was represented by a white lawyer for the sort of pragmatic reasons outlined above). The following extracts which led to counsel being called 'incompetent' are instructive:

> **BLACK COUNSEL . . .** Your honour, I am under a duty to my client to say what I am about to say. I am very, very concerned about the way your Honour has been interrupting my examination-in-chief. This is a very difficult case both for counsel and for the client, who is obviously not a British citizen. I have to concentrate on a vast number of matters in

relation to which your Honour has already used terms such as 'peripheral' and 'see where it will lead us to' in front of the jury . . . I must say that with your Honour's constant interruptions I am finding it very difficult to concentrate . . . Your Honour is not giving me the opportunity to settle the witness into giving evidence. Your Honour is not giving me the opportunity to concentrate on matters that I know go centrally to his defence and your Honour is also putting me in the unfortunate position of . . . impertinence to the bench, which is not intended . . .

JUDGE: Counsel, you will not upset me at all . . . I have made it clear to you that you shall have as much time as you want subject to the questions of wasted costs. So far, according to my timetable, it is no more than 30 minutes. Let me make it clear that counsel owes a duty to display reasonable competence. These matters in relation to the defendants business, and the like, are matters on which you have been invited by the Crown to lead. I cannot for one moment see how your failure to accept the invitation can be of any benefit to your client. All it seems to me at the moment is that by conducting a cross-examination which seems to go from point to point, without supplying your client with the documents which the court had, which you have, which the jury have, so that he is quite unable to follow your questions, as indeed I am, does not display that level of competence which I would have expected from counsel . . .

BLACK COUNSEL: If your Honour thinks I am incompetent so be it.

JUDGE: Please, I said that in my view it did not display the level of competence which I would have expected of counsel and it causes me regret to have to say it . . .

Later in this same exchange, the judge used remarks such as 'It is not for me to teach you how to do your job' and said:

. . . Your incompetence, and my comment about incompetence was directed to the fact that you were trying to examine a witness on a bundle of documents that he did not have.

As it happened, the witness who was being examined *did* have the documents in question. Nonetheless, the judge, without apologising for his own mistake, continued:

. . . I have told you, and I will repeat, that I expect counsel to show the normal level of competence expected from counsel and I have no doubt that you will do your best to achieve that and if you feel that you can lead, then the invitation as I understand it is there and I shall have to consider the position if you fail to follow the invitation and thereby take up more time than is necessary in your conduct of the case.

The jury heard the beginning of this interchange. It demonstrates the need for the anti-racist training offered to judges to go beyond knowing about other people's cultures and to include courtesy to and respect for black lawyers, whose competence should be acknowledged—as it would be in the case of white counsel—by virtue of their position as qualified, trained and often experienced advocates. They should not be belittled in public or before professional colleagues, and certainly not in front of the jury trying the case.

Chapter 6

Beatrice's Case

Of the women in the interview sample, I decided to look in greater detail at the answers given by Beatrice. These help to highlight issues discussed in earlier chapters, including the way in which black women perceive that they are treated by the criminal justice process, equality of treatment, stereotyping, assumptions about black people and various other aspects of the race-gender-class analysis outlined in *Chapter 1*. Her story also conveniently demonstrates the kind of hazards faced by black women and their sense of powerlessness when confronted by the criminal justice process.

Apart from Beatrice's personal account which is set out in the next section, what follows is based on the official court transcript and my own observations on attending the last two of the three Crown Court hearings in which she became involved.

BEATRICE'S ACCOUNT

The events leading to Beatrice's involvement with the criminal justice process and as she described them can be summarised as follows:

Beatrice went with her boyfriend to visit one of his friends who was staying at a hotel. When they arrived, both of them were arrested by customs officers. Unknown to her or her boyfriend, his friend had been arrested at Gatwick airport with packets of heroin in his stomach. The customs officers had gone to the hotel where the friend had booked a room to see if anyone was awaiting his arrival.

Beatrice protested her innocence at the time (as her boyfriend did his) and told the customs officers that she knew nothing whatsoever about the man or any drugs. While in police custody she asked if she could telephone her children (both aged below eleven years) to say where she was. Her request was denied on the ground that contacting home could prejudice the enquiry by alerting other people who might be involved in a smuggling operation.

When Beatrice's home was searched nothing of consequence was found other than a 'prayer letter'—written by Beatrice—which was inside her Bible. This was the only significant evidence in her later trial apart from the other circumstantial evidence of her visit to the hotel. The prayer letter is reproduced at the end of this chapter.

ARREST AND CHARGE

Beatrice was arrested and charged with being knowingly concerned in the evasion of the prohibition on the importation of a controlled drug, namely heroin. This offence—which concerns a Class A drug—carries a maximum sentence of life imprisonment. However, the allegation was thrown out at the magistrates' court at the committal for trial stage. Put succinctly, that court concluded that there was *insufficient evidence* for the case to be sent to the Crown Court for trial by jury. When the committal proceedings foundered in this way, the prosecutor obtained a voluntary bill of indictment for Beatrice's arraignment to face trial in the Crown Court (a legitimate but comparatively unusual method of securing trial at the Crown Court, though not a matter from which any truly valid conclusions can be drawn in the context of discrimination or differential treatment). Beatrice was re-arrested the same day.

THE PROCEEDINGS

Including the abortive committal proceedings, Beatrice took part in a total of four hearings before she was ultimately convicted. The offence is not a palatable one, nor a natural basis upon which to invite sympathy or attention to her opinions, but this cannot be allowed to obscure the question whether she was treated in the same way that a white suspect or defendant would have been—or whether her explanations and protestations of innocence were given the same attention or credence as those of someone not tainted by white people's assumptions about black women. There were three Crown Court hearings as follows:

- at the first Beatrice was found guilty by an *all-white* jury (a decision later set aside on appeal when a fresh trial was ordered);

- at the second, where the jury was made up half of *black* people and half of *white* people, it could not reach a verdict; and

- at the third, where the jury was *all-white*, she was again found guilty.

Whilst, legally speaking, nothing can gainsay the decision of the jury in the third—and technically speaking the only valid—trial, Beatrice was angry and bitter at the way she felt she had been treated from arrest to conviction and the persistence with which the case was pursued in the light of what seemed to be flimsy evidence.

THE CROWN COURT TRIAL(S)

At the time of our discussions, Beatrice had served almost two years of a seven year prison sentence and was awaiting being deported. It was her first involvement with the criminal law—both she and her co-defendant were of good character and it was accepted by the prosecutor that they had never been in trouble with the law before either in this country or abroad. In her own mind, she had no doubt that racism was rife in the criminal justice process and that she had been treated unfairly: because she was black and foreign (even though living in Britain at the time of the offence).

Before Beatrice could be convicted, the jury would need to be satisfied beyond reasonable doubt (the standard of proof in criminal proceedings) that she realised that a prohibited drug was involved and that she was knowingly concerned in its importation. At all stages she denied *any* involvement with the alleged courier of the drugs or *any* knowledge of the drug or its importation. This she repeated at her trial. For all practical purposes, everything therefore turned on the interpretation placed by the jury on the visit to the hotel and the prayer letter, and this was accepted by prosecuting counsel. There was no independent or direct evidence against her co-defendant either.

Central to the case, the prosecutor called an expert witness—a white British bishop who had lived in Nigeria for 15 years in colonial times among the Ibo—to give his opinion about the true meaning of the letter.

A conflict of expert opinion

The white British bishop said that Ibo were deep believers in written charms. In his experience they would put a charm on someone and, referring to the words in the prayer, 'I'm not afraid', he said he had repeatedly come across this kind of charm and that, overall, the letter was a typical charm or 'juju', a prayer for wealth to be obtained by various means. It was, he concluded, concerned with the importation of heroin—about seeking God's help in smuggling heroin and designed to ensure Beatrice did not get caught.

To counter this, the defence called a minister from the Pentecostal church as an expert witness. He was a black man of Jamaican origin, although he lived in Britain. The black minister said that the letter was *not* a charm *nor* a 'juju', but a prayer letter which was common among Pentecostal members. It was typical of such letters and 'asked for deliverance'.

In his summing up to the jury, the judge emphasised how the bishop had lived in Nigeria for 15 years among the Ibo and that he spoke the Ibo language. He also pointed out that the expert witness for the defence had 'recently qualified' as a minister and that he was employed by London Transport. Another statement by the judge that 'maybe the minister's evidence was what he had been told by the defendant' may have implied that the minister was not capable of thinking for himself. The jury of six black people and six white people failed to reach a verdict and there was consequently a retrial.

The retrial
At the retrial—now a third Crown Court ordeal for Beatrice—similar testimony was relied on. The white bishop continued to refer to the prayer letter as a 'charm' or 'juju', stating:

> . . . in my opinion, (the prayer letter) is a typical charm or juju against discovery and to protect the bearer and their immediate associates. The writing is couched in biblical language in order to give it power but the language is changed and gives a particular emphasis. An example of this is the part in the prayer which says 'My God gives me power to be rich. The Lord will give me the treasures of the Kingdom of Darkness and hidden riches of secret places of that Kingdom.

This was, he said:

> . . . a typical reference to the manner in which drugs are commonly brought from Nigeria to the United Kingdom. The quotation . . . 'For the wealth of the wicked is for me the just that I may know' . . . refers in my opinion to the profit that can be gained from the smuggling of drugs.

He continued that the words

> I am not afraid of them be it customs, immigration officers, police both in London and in Nigeria, devil and his cohorts wicked spirit of any order or class spirit of heroin for the Lord my God is with me.

and its language were typical of a charm to protect against discovery. In his opinion, the same was true of the sentence beginning 'Nobody searcheth me or my baggage'. His final conclusion was:

> It may be difficult for someone living in England to understand the power and depth of belief that a charm such as this would have for someone coming from a Nigerian culture. To any Nigerian the reality of the world of the spirit is quite strong, if not stronger than the world of factual and material things . . . In any enterprise it is therefore important to the Nigerian to protect themselves against bad or malign spirits or influences which might be adverse to the enterprise.

During cross-examination by defence counsel, substantial parts of the letter were accepted by the white bishop as capable of perfectly innocent or alternative interpretations to those put forward by him and consistent with Beatrice's protestations of innocence and the Pentecostal faith, but he refused to place a virtuous interpretation on these items himself. An example of this aspect of the cross-examination can be demonstrated by the following extract:

Q 'Hidden riches' is capable of being construed as a reference to those souls yet to be saved. They are potential riches for the kingdom of God, but they are not yet actual riches because they have yet to come within that Kingdom?

A All that I can say — as you say, you are pressing me on this — is that is not my interpretation. It is not the way I would read it.

Q The Pentecostal Evangelist faith is a very zealous faith, is it not?

A Yes.

Q Zealous, in particular, in saving souls?

A Yes.

Q Souls not yet saved are regarded as souls held by the Devil are they not, in the very literal interpretation the Pentecostalist commonly places upon it?

A That interpretation can be put on it. Yes, it can.

Q The souls of the unbelievers are regarded as 'ripe', if you will forgive that expression, for being brought into the Kingdom of God? They are potential recruits?

91

A   One can put any interpretation on it. I mean, I can only say what I read the total thing to mean. If one abstracts individual sentences and says, 'Could another interpretation not be put on this'? The answer very often is 'Yes.' But it is not the interpretation, reading it in the whole, that I put on it, I am afraid . . .

It also is worth noting that at the second of the Crown Court trials, this outcome had occurred, in one instance, with the judge's intervention:

Q   . . . if customs, immigration and the police had previously caused a person difficulty or distress, the belief will be not that those people were themselves evil, but that the Devil was employing them to do his evil work through their offices?

A   No; I am sorry, I do not think I can place that interpretation on it.

Q   If the person has had a great deal of distress brought into their life as a result of contact, innocent or otherwise, with heroin, it is entirely possible that somebody in his faith would name that devil in order to ask God to cast it out, is it not?

A   Yes, it is possible.

Judge (Intervening)

In the terms in which it is done in this letter? If somebody was trying to cast out heroin, because it has affected some part of their life, would you see it written in the way in which it is written here in the context in which it is here?

A   No, your Honour, I would not.

It is fair to say that the judge in question did point out that, at the end of the day, it was a matter for the jury, not the bishop, to decide the status of the letter and what it meant, but by then a message (albeit possibly wrong) may have registered with some members of the jury that the judge may not have thought much of the answers being elicited in cross-examination, and that he preferred answers which were more telling as against the defendant.

In his evidence for the defence, the black Pentecostal evangelist minister disagreed with the white bishop's interpretations. According to him:

It is the custom of many Pentecostal Christians to write prayer letters as a means of asking God to act and help on their behalf for the goodness of personal deliverances or deliverance for others. One of the fundamental beliefs as a Pentecostal is to take the promises of God literally and spiritually.

He went on to explain that the prayer letter was a typical letter from someone who had experienced problems in the past and that in his opinion it was *not* a prayer to protect from discovery of illegal acts or operations. The fact that Beatrice, in the letter, mentions her pastor as well as her husband, he interpreted as meaning that:

She wants her husband to be with her in her faith and that she wants her pastor to be stronger or to continue in the faith. In the Pentecostal faith we pray for brothers and sisters who are in the faith and pastors who are leading to lead with simplicity and honesty . . . A pastor would not be included in the letter if its intention was for evil or to avoid discovery.

He said that Beatrice had stated that she was not 'afraid' of people or circumstances because God would help her through her troubles. She was asking for help to see her through a difficult period and to cast out the evils from her life:

Many people who have encountered great problems are afraid and use these phrases (as in the prayer letter) to give them strength to face their fear. It is not a prayer against discovery, it is a prayer to give strength to carry on.

Where the prayer letter refers to 'my people' and 'my brothers', the minister considered that it was praying for the whole world to be engulfed in faith. His conclusion was that:

Asking for riches to spread the word of God, to give or to help to instruct in the word of God . . . is common to many churches, not only the Pentecostal—it is not a reference to profit that can be made from importing drugs.

Beatrice's evidence
Whilst under arrest and when she later gave evidence in court after electing to go into the witness box and to explain to the jury on oath the meaning of the prayer so far as she was concerned, Beatrice described the letter as 'a prayer of deliverance and renewal of my life.' She was 'very religious' and of the Pentecostal faith (she had set up bible classes in prison and letters were read out in court written by

93

people on her behalf about the nature and extent of her religious beliefs).

Beatrice explained that her husband had been arrested and charged with possession and supply of heroin about a year before she was arrested and charged with the present offence. He was now serving a prison sentence which had caused problems for their marriage and they were now separated. Beatrice believed that he was involved with drugs and that this was a result of being influenced by evil spirits. She said that she wanted him delivered from this problem and had written the prayer letter to exorcise the evil influence of heroin. She had written it partly due to police harassment she was suffering due to her husband's activities. She said that '. . . after my husband's arrest the police would come to my house at any time to search for things and sometimes take pictures of me and my children without prior warning.'

She said that where the prayer mentions protection from 'customs, immigration and police' it was because she feared the blacking of her name as a result of her husband's conviction. She also said that after her husband had been arrested and imprisoned she had started an export and import business to support her children. A customs officer had been to Nigeria to verify this and found no evidence to link her with drugs and no wrongdoing. The customs officer also investigated and 'cleared' the business of co-defendant. In court it was said that he was a successful businessman with a legitimate net profit of £42,000 a year.

The summing up

The essential features of the judge's summing up to the jury are as follows:

> The Crown called, in order to help you (the jury) — to understand the true meaning of this letter, the bishop — He is a bishop and the defence expert witness happens to be a minister in the Pentecostal Church and also a bus driver. It might be tempting to say that it is a bit unfair, bishop obviously outranks him — The bishop is an Anglican, not a Pentecostal but he does have as he told you, at least 15 years of actual experience of ministry in Nigeria and amongst Ibo people. He (the bishop) says this is a letter from his experience of those people practising their Pentecostal religion designed to protect her in her search not for spiritual riches but material riches through the evil trade in heroin. In general the bishop said that although it may seem paradoxical, it is not uncommon, certainly not unheard of, for these prayer letters, apparently couched in religious terms and indeed no doubt penned by persons who believe in the power of their God, to none the less use them to ask for protection from doing something

very unchristian which is really the opposite of what the minister was seeking to say to you.

He continued:

It is right to say, first of all on the plus side, the minister is himself a Pentecostal, although his background is in the West Indies, in particular in Jamaica, and he has absolutely no experience of Nigeria or the Ibo people. So he was speaking from a Pentecostal point of view, but a Pentecostal point of view from either West Indian or English points of view.

The jury retired at 3.32 p.m. and returned with their verdict at 5.17 p.m.—'guilty' in respect of both defendants. There was no pre-sentence report pursuant to the Criminal Justice Act 1991. The judge stated that the probation officers at the prison had said they could not produce one for Beatrice because of pressure of work. Sentencing went ahead without one.

SOME ISSUES RAISED BY BEATRICE'S CASE

Having followed Beatrice's case closely and discussed it at length with a number of people, I believe that the events throw some light on extra-legal factors which may affect decisions to arrest, charge, convict and sentence black women:

- if the prayer letter at the centre of the case had been found on a white person it is unlikely that it would have been given credence without further substantial evidence. But the popular image persists of black people being involved in 'mumbo jumbo', charms, superstition and 'black magic'.

- the judges in both of the last two Crown Court hearings appear to have sought to discredit or undermine the evidence of the black minister who one of them described as 'working for London Transport' and the other as a 'bus driver'. In the interests of avoiding prejudice, this seemingly gratuitous information might have been better avoided altogether, its only real effect being to undermine the evidence of the minister, the implication being that he was not as well qualified or suited to the task of interpretation as the bishop, or that he lacked authenticity or was not clever or intelligent enough for his understanding of theology to count. There were no counterbalancing comments to the effect that the white bishop did not appear to have a particularly high opinion of the African people he had served for 15 years—in respect of whom he uses what many black people would regard as 'racist' and 'contemptuous' remarks—in somewhat outdated, colonial times! He seems to have remained prejudiced in his personal views about the Ibo. Why did the judge choose to give the bishop a fair wind rather than to point out, for example, that it is unlikely a *white* person would understand and relate to Nigerian culture as well as a *black* minister, albeit Jamaican? He simply assumed that the white bishop is capable of being an expert on black people!

- the fact that the bishop lived in Nigeria during colonial times would say a lot about his stereotyping of black people. In that era, black people had no say and were ill-treated by their white masters who simply assumed white superiority.

- the entire proceedings seem to disclose a view of black people as primitive simply because their culture is different to that of the dominant culture of the white majority in Britain. It is nowhere commented on, for example, by the judge that many black people in Britain are exceedingly religious. (One of the ways some black people respond to racism in this country is by turning to the evangelical type churches).

- it is also worth considering the extent to which Beatrice may have been viewed by white jury members as someone whose behaviour or lifestyle were inappropriate to her role as a woman: see, generally, *Chapter 2*. Arguably, this may also have affected the decision to dispense with a PSR and possibly the length of her sentence. The events seem to be littered with examples of where Beatrice may have been sanctioned for 'inappropriate behaviour'. As argued in *Chapter 2*, black women are seen as having a propensity for criminal behaviour which is not matched in the case of white women.

Beatrice's sentence of seven year's imprisonment and the associated recommendation that she be deported afterwards presented her with a dilemma which many foreign black people face. She protested her innocence and wanted to appeal, but withdrew her application when it was pointed out to her that if she did not she would have to remain in prison for the decision of the appeal court. She was missing her children and did not know how they were coping. At first the prosecutor said that she could not be released unless her co-defendant had dropped his appeal as well, but with the intervention of an organization which works with foreign women in prison, she was later released, even though her co-defendant was pressing ahead with his own appeal

PRAYER LETTER

The prayer letter which served as the main exhibit in Beatrice's case is reproduced overleaf.

The prayer letter, which was typed but corrected by hand, read as follows (set out as in the original, including the spacing, insertions and incorrect spellings, save that the phrases 'spirit of heroin' and 'my husband Frank' each appeared in a loosely drawn box as opposed to simply being underlined):

My God gives me power to be rich.

I that wait upon the Lord shall renew my strenght, I shall

mount up with wings as eagles, I shall run and not be weary

and I shall walk free and not faint. for the <u>tree</u> beareth her fruit
                                              Jesus
. the fig tree and the vine / do yield their strength, I

rejioce in the Lord for he has given me former rain moderately

and will cause it to come down on me, the former rain and the

Latter rain in the f<u>or</u>th month then the abundance of God's

blessing will overflow in my Life for the days are at hand to

the effect of every promise and vision in now for I The Lord
of the abundance rain is here   the kingdom
has spoken/for the   Lord will give me the treasure of darkness
of   of that kingdom
and hidden riches in secret places,   for the wealth of the

wicked is for me the first that I know that My Lord which

I call by name is My God of Abundance and prosperity. Praise
God.
          (page 2)
I am strong and of Good Courage I fear not, <u>I am not afraid</u>

<u>of them, be it Customs, immigration officers, police both in</u>

<u>London and in Nigeria, devil and his cohorts,</u> wicked spirit

of any order of class, <u>spirit of heroin</u>, for the Lord my God

is with me. He will not fail me or forsake me, It's He that

go before me, He is with me He will not fail me neighter

                           No body

forsake me. I fear not neighter will I be dismayed. For he has
searcheth me or my baggage   and about my
made a hedge about \ and about my household and about my people
baggages   me
and about the body of Christ and about my brothers and about

                           including my

my pastor and about all that I have on every side. He has blessed
children and <u>my husband Frank</u>
the work of my hands and my substance is increased in the Land.

I have travailed and given birth to this and many more and they

had manifested in Jesus name.

Amen

Chapter 7

Black Women in Prison

The number of women in prison in England and Wales has risen sharply, the rate of increase being double that for male prisoners. The total prison population rose from 40,606 at the end of 1992 to 59,157 on 7 March 1997. As this book goes to press, a Home Office study reports that it is expected to rise by another 19,200 by 2005, moving towards the 75,000 mark, with a further increase of 11,000 by 2011[1]. In the background to this is one of the toughest and most politicised law and order election campaigns in modern times. Proportionately, women offenders have suffered a worse fate than men offenders. Whereas the number of male prisoners rose by 29 per cent over the three year period to December 1995 (from 39,253 to 50,606) the number of women prisoners rose by 57 per cent (1,353 to 2,125).

The mid-1995 figures show that 24 per cent of the female prison population is from minority ethnic groups and 20 per cent of female prisoners classified as black (see the further comments in *Chapter 1*). The breakdown of the total female prison population by ethnic origin as at 30 June 1994 shows that of the 1,804 women in prison on that date, 1,355 (75 per cent) were white; 370 (21 per cent) were black; 27 (1 per cent) were South Asian; 52 (3 per cent) were 'Chinese or other'; and two were unrecorded. In total, 25 per cent of female prisoners were from minority ethnic groups: 12 per cent British, 13 per cent foreign.

In 1994, 3,714 women were remanded in custody, the average number on remand at any one time being 490. The *Prison Statistics* show that just 29 per cent of these women subsequently returned to prison as sentenced prisoners (compared with 44 per cent of men on remand). Seventy-one per cent of such women were acquitted, given non-custodial sentences or the case not proceeded with. [2]

Prison Service staffing and initiatives
So far as prison staff are concerned, five members of the Prison Service's 1,020 governor grades (0.49 per cent) and 354 out of 19,325

---

[1] At the time of going to press this information was reported upon in *The Times*, 4 April 1997. The same report indicates that the number of women in prison is expected to rise to 3,500 by 2005.

[2] HMSO, 1996.

prison officers (2.4 per cent) are from minority ethnic groups.[3] The Service has developed a comprehensive race relations policy. In individual prisons, race relations liaison officers have been appointed and race relations management teams established to implement the Service's policies.[4] A *Race Relations Manual* was introduced in 1991 (see under the heading Racism) later in this chapter. Governors are required to set targets for the recruitment of prison officers from minority ethnic groups. Training on race issues has been reviewed and updated, and an offence of racially discriminatory behaviour is now included in the prison service staff disciplinary code.

ASPECTS OF WOMEN'S IMPRISONMENT

The 2,073 women in prison on 23 February 1996 constituted four per cent of the total prison population. Most of them were not violent and many had committed relatively minor crimes. In fact, in 1994, 33 per cent of the annual female prison receptions (1,454) were for fine default. Apart from anything hidden within uncategorised offences, of the remaining women prisoners, only 514 (17 per cent) had been convicted of the type of offence which might pose some risk to the public: violent offences, sexual offences or robbery (an offence involving violence or threats of violence). The rest were in prison for drugs offences (287), theft or handling stolen goods (1,125), fraud and forgery (265), burglary (137), or uncategorised offences or where the offence was not recorded (761).

The seeds for the rise in the imprisonment of women were sown in the 1970s and 1980s. The National Association of Probation Officers asserted that there had been '. . . almost a fourfold increase in twelve years' in the total number of women sentenced to imprisonment *annually*, from about 800 in 1974 to around 3000 in 1986. That increase occurred against the background of a *decrease* in the total number of women sentenced by the courts for indictable offences.[5]

A striking feature of the current escalation is that women prisoners tend to have few previous convictions or in many cases none at all. Thus, for example, in 1994, as many as 60 per cent of women prisoners had two or fewer previous convictions, including 20 per cent with none. By comparison, 33 per cent of sentenced male prisoners for

---

[3] 'Race Discrimination and the Criminal Justice System', NAPO and ABPO, 1996.
[4] 'Race and Criminal Justice', Penal Affairs Consortium, September 1996.
[5] NAPO, 1989

whom previous convictions were known had two or fewer. Only 16 per cent had no previous convictions.[6]

Psychiatric disorder

A survey of 262 sentenced women prisoners and 1,751 male prisoners, published in 1994, found that a higher proportion of women prisoners had personality disorders (18 per cent compared with 10 per cent of men), neurotic disorders (18 per cent compared with 10 per cent), mental handicap (6 per cent compared with 2 per cent) and problems of substance abuse (26 per cent compared with 12 per cent). Approximately 2 per cent of both groups suffered from psychoses.

Fifty seven per cent of women had more than one diagnosis compared with 38 per cent of men.[7]

Approximately two per cent of both groups suffered from psychoses. Fifty-seven per cent of women had more than one diagnosis compared with 38 per cent of men.

Forty-five per cent of women prisoners had had contact with psychiatric services before their prison sentence compared with 36 per cent of men. Thirty-two per cent of women reported deliberate self-harm on at least one occasion during their life compared with 12 per cent of men, although the percentage of each group reporting self-harm in prison was similar. The researchers concluded that this finding '. . . does not take account of gender differences in the frequency of self-harm'.

Aspects of the way in which the police use mental health powers to ensure that black women are taken to a 'place of safety' are mentioned in *Chapter 3*.

Distance from home

Because there are fewer women's prisons (14 in total), women are more likely to be held at a distance from their homes, with all that this entails for family ties, visits by relatives and children, and probation officers or social workers from their home area. Mounting pressure on accommodation has meant that less attention is now paid to these social or rehabilitative factors than the immediate task of locating available space.[8]

---

[6] 'The Imprisonment of Women: Some Facts and Figures', Penal Affairs Consortium, March 1996.

[7] 'A Criminological and Psychiatric Survey of Women Serving a Prison Sentence', Maden, Swinton and Gunn, *British Journal of Criminology*, Vol. 34 No. 2, 1994.

[8] 'The Imprisonment of Women: Some Facts and Figures', Penal Affairs Consortium, March 1996.

Foreign women

As already indicated, a significant proportion of women prisoners are foreign nationals, often serving sentences for drugs offences, including importation into the United Kingdom. In addition to the problems usually associated with imprisonment, such women—who are often young black women—face additional difficulties in coping with a different culture, language problems, isolation, lack of family contact, and acute anxiety about the welfare of children who are either in care or in poverty-stricken conditions in their home country.

Up to a third of women in prison in England and Wales are drug couriers from other countries who will be deported after serving a prison sentence.

(Discrimination in custody in relation to black women and women from other ethnic minorities also includes, particularly for foreign women, a paucity of basic information in their own language and lack of a comprehensive or always adequate interpreting service,[9] poor catering for special diets, and failure to access education classes because foreigners, above all black women, are problematic in this regard.)

Short sentences

Many black women are in prison for short sentences (less than 12 months). Had they been men (certainly white men), this group would have been targeted for community service or probation, the latter possibly with enhanced varieties of conditions attached to the order. Generally speaking, as at 1991:

> In spite of government efforts to reduce the use of custody for non-violent offences, there was evidence . . . that many women had been sent to prison for short periods for offences of dishonesty . . . In many of these cases and following consideration of the records, it was not apparent what benefit could accrue to society from the prison sentence of a few months' duration.[10]

Black women's special difficulties

All women in prison experience difficulties, but for black women there are additional burdens which they encounter on remand, during sentence or on release. They experience discrimination in prison in many ways. (The prison system, in common with other parts of the criminal justice process, was established and designed by and for men

---

[9] *Interpreters and the Legal Process*, Colin J and Morris R, Waterside Press, 1996.
[10] H.M. Inspectorate Report, 1991 p.58.

and by and for white people. This is evident at all levels: from life-sentence prisoners[11] and services for mentally disordered offenders[12] to the lack of appropriate provision for women during sentence and on release.[13]

LABELLING THEORY → NOT BENEFICIAL

Stereotypes

The stereotype of the black woman mentioned in *Chapter 1*—for many prison officers a negative stereotype—affects the way black women are treated. Wilson states that:

> We (black women) are . . . mad and we commit crime and we sponge off the system . . . etc. Black women are not even allowed the patronising treatment of being seen as 'fragile little creatures' who must be protected. We are supposed to be able to cope in whatever situations arise. In prison, for example, black women are often viewed as so violent that they have to be dealt with by male officers . . . [14]

Racism

The *Race Relations Manual* for prison officers mentioned at the start of this chapter indicates that racist behaviour or abuse is a serious disciplinary matter. Launching the manual in 1991, Angela Rumbold, then Home Office minister with responsibility for prisons, said:

> We all know that discrimination does still occur in our prisons, against both prisoners and staff. Some is overt, perhaps racial abuse of prisoners or harassment of ethnic minority officers. While some is unintentional, like stereotyping which leads to false assumptions about a person's behaviour . . . I . . . firmly believe that prisoners . . . regardless of colour, race or religion, should be treated with equality, humanity and respect.[15]

The minister emphasised race and colour without mentioning gender, as if racial discrimination is not sometimes—as argued throughout this book—linked to gender or class discrimination. Although it would appear that the minister recognised that religion can be connected to race, the Home Office has consistently refused to recognise Rastafarianism as a religion, thereby exposing those black women Rastafarians to a form of institutionalised discrimination.

---

[11] 'Women Lifers: Assessing the Experience', Player E, Cropwood Series, No. 19, 1988.

[12] 'Review of Health and Social Services for Mentally Disordered Offenders' (The 'Reed Report'), HMSO, 1992.

[13] 'Post-Release Experiences of Female Prisoners', Wilkinson C, Cropwood Series, No 19, 1988.

[14] 'Black Female Prisoners and Political Awareness', Black Women in Prison, 1985.

[15] NACRO, 1992.

Genders and Player found that some prison officers held racist views and that the prevailing perception of most prison officers was that Asians are 'clean', 'hard-working' and 'no-trouble' whilst blacks are 'arrogant', 'hostile to authority' and have 'chips on their shoulders'. Race relations officers sometimes had a difficult time with their colleagues—one was referred to as the 'Sambo-Samaritan'.[16]

Black women prisoners may not report incidents and keep silent because they believe there is nothing to gain by complaining and they do not want to be viewed by staff as 'trouble-makers'. Many did not know that there were specialist race relations staff.

A report by the Oxford University Centre for Criminological Research found a wide gap between the low number of racial incidents recorded by the prison service and the large number reported to them and confirms that black people in prison are at a disadvantage, and subjected to racism because of their skin colour, including: victimisation by prisoners and staff, unfair treatment over access to facilities and education, racial abuse and harassment, unfair discipline, bullying and assault.[17]

Applications and petitions

Offences *against* prisoners should be treated as seriously as offences *by* prisoners. The chain of communication for complaints (known as applications) starts with wing officers (i.e. the prison officer in charge of the prison wing or a comparable section of a prison), who are often those against whom the complaints were made, so that not all serious complaints reach the prison governor or the Home Office by way of petition.

Prison discipline

Black women in prison who are British nationals, and even *citizens* of the United Kingdom, are under constant pressure to prove that they are not otherwise. Some were referred to as model prisoners, but others were resentful and receive punishments in the form of loss of privileges, fines, solitary confinement, etc. Padel and Stevenson state that:

> Women prisoners are disciplined more than twice as often as men. In 1986, 3.6 offences were punished per head of the female prison population as against 1.6 per head of the male prison population. A much higher proportion of prison rule offences committed by women fall into the

---

[16] *Race Relations in Prisons*, Genders E and Player E, Clarendon Press, 1989.

[17] 'Reported and Unreported Racial Incidents in Prisons', 1994.

'mutiny or violence' category than by men, which is surprising given that all the major prison riots have occurred in men's prison. [18]

Prison jobs

Seemingly, black people can be systematically discriminated against and allocated the worst jobs—labouring and cleaning, whilst the better jobs are given to white prisoners. A South East London probation officer noted that although black women who served long sentences for drug offences were

> . . . almost all dignified, respectful and unworldly . . . (they) tend to get all the shit jobs in the prison, like working in the kitchens from 6.00 a.m. to 5.00 p.m., but they don't complain because it keeps them occupied. They prefer it because they don't have time to think about their families. In the end they have nothing. [19]

Alexander v Home Office[20] also emphasises the problem some black prisoners may face in this and other areas where discretion is exercised in prison. In Wandsworth and Parkhurst prisons, Alexander's assessment report and induction report contained the following remarks:

> He displays the usual traits associated with people of his ethnic background being arrogant, suspicious of staff, anti-authority, devious and possessing a very large, chip on his shoulder which he will find very difficult to remove if he carries on the way he is doing . . . He is an arrogant person who is suspicious of staff and totally anti-authority.

> He has been described as a violent man with a very large chip on his shoulder which he will have great difficult in removing. He shows the anti-authoritarian arrogance that seems to be common in most coloured inmates.

The prisoner was awarded damages of £1,000. Some black women prisoners may also get 'shit jobs'. For example, a black woman ex-prisoner complained that:

> Most of the jobs they give you (in prison) are to make you into a good housewife: cleaning, scrubbing, knitting and sewing. I hear that men get

---

[18] *Insiders: Women's Experience of Prisons*, Padel U and Stevenson P, Virago, 1988: 10.
[19] 'To the Slaughter', Roberts Y, New Statesman and Society, 13 October 1989.
[20] 1988 WLR 968.

carpentry jobs, machine jobs, and all those interesting pursuits and studies.[21]

Generally speaking research into work done by women prisoners has tended to focus on work allocated to women in general and therefore has not analysed how racism can play a part. Although most of the problems identified, including that of isolation from family and children, affect foreign black men as well, the situation of black women is compounded by the finding that the foreign black women keep themselves to themselves more than the foreign black men in prison.[22]

A profile of women prisoners
A Home Office research study based on interviews with 200 women in three prisons between January 1993 and January 1994 found that:

> The women in this sample were broadly typical of female prisoners elsewhere. They were generally young, criminally unsophisticated, and were mainly in prison for property offences. Over 40 per cent were mothers of dependent children and nearly half of these were single parents. Nearly 60 per cent of the women said that they were living solely on benefits prior to their imprisonment . . .

> Almost half of the women reported having used drugs, prior to their imprisonment and more than half of these women associated their offending with their drug use. Nearly one quarter described themselves as having a drink problem, two thirds of these women also reported drug use.[23]

The study also notes, among other things, that nearly 25 per cent reported harming themselves, 50 per cent having been physically abused and nearly one third being sexually abused. Over 40 per cent complained of difficulties maintaining contact with their children, especially towards their release date.

INTERVIEWS

I talked to the women about their experiences in prison, their relationships with prison officers and prison life in general. Over two thirds of them were in open prisons, two in closed prisons and two

---

[21] *Channel 4*, 19 September 1991.
[22] 'Drug Couriers', Green P, Howard League, 1991.
[23] 'Managing the Needs of Female Prisoners', Morris, Wilkinson, Tisi, Woodrow and Rockley, Home Office, 1995.

under probation service supervision (but had served prison terms in the past). Despite the obvious disadvantages they would face in the future as black women and now ex-prisoners, many of them, especially the older women, had decided to spend their prison sentence as constructively as they could and 'to do something about their situation'.

Education and prison jobs

Most of the women felt that education was a way to a better life, even if provision was diminishing and, so it appeared to them, geared mainly to white women and English-speakers. Some *were* able to take courses and were planning to use the resulting certificates to get a job on release:

> I have spent my time in prison constructively, and have done a few City and Guilds courses. When I leave here all I want is a job and to start all over again. (Angela)

> I go to college outside prison and am doing a secretarial course — I am sitting for my exams next month. I really want to pass it. I find education in prison to be only basic. (Dawn)

> I'm doing a hairdressing course at college outside prison so that when I go out I can have my own business and look after my children. (Geraldine)

In open prison it seems that all the women were encouraged to take up education regardless of the colour of their skin. Half were attending classes and were looking at this as their last opportunity to improve their job prospects on release. It follows that half were *not* attending classes, for whatever reason. A black woman prison teacher I interviewed for another project said that she never had any black women in her class and each time she asked about the black women who had put forward their names to attend she was told there were not enough officers to escort them. Again, it may be that black women do not get places because of preconceived notions that they are problematic.

Some of the women complained about lack of continuity of education provision when transferred to another prison:

> There is no continuity — so if you are moved from one prison to another there is no guarantee that in that prison they do that course. For example, where I was before I came here I was doing painting and decorating there, and here they do not do it. (Karen)

The women said that in the closed prisons where they had been sent before being transferred, it was difficult for them to attend education classes as there were not enough prison officers to escort them:

I'm doing an information and technology—City and Guilds—course. I'm hoping to pass it. (Dawn)

I'm starting a course in catering in September. I'm looking forward to it. (Karen)

Those women with children in prison appeared to have practical problems with attending classes regularly:

I attend home economics classes but sometimes I have to miss the class as we take it in turns to look after the children. (Doreen)

I cannot attend education classes because I'm having difficulties in studying at night as the lights are turned off at 10 p.m. and the dim light comes on—this is affecting my eyes . . . I want to study because I now realise that it is time for me to do something . . . qualify in something so that when I go out I can get a job. I really want to do a child care course so that I can work with children. (Miriam)

Those who were worrying about their children at home not having enough to live on tended to work rather than attend education classes as this meant having more money, however little. The job allocation system was considered fair in one open prison, even though most of the jobs were in the kitchen or gardening and the women were pleased to be allowed to attend a nearby Pentecostal church which 'helped to keep their spirits up'. Two were doing what they described as 'fulfilling' community work.

Prison officers

All the women expressed displeasure at the way prison officers treated black women prisoners in the closed prison (where each of them had been at some time or other during their sentence). They were more critical of younger officers, for example.

You can only talk to the older prison officers. The older ones are better— the younger ones abuse their power. (Cora)

Ten of the women felt that prison officers were fair but had to look 'tough' and so behaved differently in front of their colleagues. The women felt isolated or used:

Some of them (prison officers) rarely talk to you. When you are in prison what you need is someone you can talk to, someone who can listen to your problems. (Judith)

Some officers were not interested in your problems, but gossip. They only wanted you to tell them about other inmates. (Lorraine)

In that prison I would say all the prison officers are the same regardless of colour. You just had to do what you were told so you were not put on report. (Margaret)

Twelve of the women felt that foreign black women were subjected to harsher treatment. For example, Karen said:

Foreign black women have it tough in prisons . . . some of them can't speak English and the prison officers don't bother to explain the rules to them. Most of these women don't know their rights.

Similarly, Maxine and Miriam, respectively, said:

I felt that they (prison officers) were making their rules as they went along. Black women were treated differently – in most cases it was black women who were put on report.

I had to do everything they said because I was missing my children. I wanted to be out as soon as possible. After all, I was only there for failing to pay a fine.

Josephine, talking about her experience at a closed prison, said:

The prison where I was taken to first time, the prison officers there gave me a hard time. I went to ask for some breakfast for my son and happened to mention about variety of food for children – and the prison officer said what do you know about choices – and went as far as saying black people live in huts. I kept quiet because I did not want to be put on report.

There were some views among some of the women I interviewed in open prison who seemed reasonably happy with the treatment they were receiving:

The officers here are good . . . you can't complain – we all get on well. (Dawn)

111

They are easy going here—if you don't bother them (prison officers) they won't bother you. There are one or two odd ones though—I wish we had at least one black prison or probation officer. (Jane)

Here prison officers are OK. The food is better than other prisons. There are no black officers though. (Lorraine)

It would appear that a prison officer who is prepared to listen to women's problems is seen as a good officer:

Prison officers here are good. They have time to sit with you and listen to your problems . . . You do get one or two odd ones. (Fumi)

In my earlier study, interviewees felt that women in prison who self-mutilate do so because officers do not have time to listen to women's problems. Others said:

When you are in there a lot of things get you down. Women worry about their children, about losing their homes. The officers should sit down and talk to them. (Miriam)

Thus the women felt that prison officers should have more time to talk and to listen to their problems, and this was seen as a way of reducing tensions and problems, including self-harm.

All the women talked about privileges and how they could be withdrawn for trivial matters. Sixteen of them felt that racism played a part.

I feel if an officer takes a dislike to you or if she is racist . . . you have your privileges withdrawn more. The officers abuse their power. (Jackie)

The women also felt that they were treated like children:

. . . to keep on their (the officers') right side you have to behave like a child . . . and do as you are told kind of thing. (Maureen)

Prison discipline
Another problem which was raised by the women was being put 'on report' for minor things. This happened to all women but black women felt it was happening to them even more. Judith was not happy with the advice she had received from the prison governor whilst in prison. She said:

112

I absconded when I was first sent to prison—this was a closed prison. I absconded because I was missing my children. I had four children at that time—I got pregnant whilst out. The governor at that prison said 'I'm giving you motherly advice and you must have an abortion—and she was telling the nurses to make me make my mind up quickly as time was running out. I did not plan it—it happened—it was an accident. I just could not bring myself to kill a human being. At times I was confused and used to cry a lot.

At the time I interviewed Judith, she was pregnant with her sixth child and was expecting the baby the following month. This was her second pregnancy whilst in prison and she was in prison with her child. She said that:

When I went home on leave I got pregnant for the second time . . . Its my luck. I've been crying ever since I got pregnant. The prison officers here are supportive. My boyfriend is supportive and he comes to visit. (Judith)

Some writers have considered that penal policy continues to be dominated by beliefs about women which were pre-eminent at the turn of the century and which largely reflect the moralistic theories about normality and deviance in women. Dobash, Dobash and Gutteridge found that women in prison are more closely observed, controlled and punished than men, often for more trivial offences.[24] A report by H. M. Inspector of Prisons endorses this.[25] Offences against prison discipline and punishment demonstrate a six per cent rise in such offences in 1991 for women. The level was the highest since 1986, and each year the figure has been consistently higher than for men.[26]

Racism

One woman who was refused temporary release at the closed prison when her mother was ill in hospital because she was a deportee said:

There is racism in prison . . . The law says one thing and in prison they have their own law. What I found at that prison was that black women were not given temporary release but foreign non-black deportees were allowed to go outside prison to attend college or work. (Dawn)

And others:

---

[24] *The Imprisonment of Women*, Dobash RE, Dobash RP and Gutteridge S, Basil Blackwell, 1986.

[25] Report of H M Inspector of Prisons 1988, HMSO, 1989.

[26] *Offences Against Prison Discipline and Punishments 1991*, Home Office, 1992.

They are horrible to foreign black women, reminding them all the time about where they come from and saying how lucky they are to have this and that. (Jackie)

The way they talk to you it's like you are nothing—like you are dirty. (Miriam)

I was put on report for what they called aggressive behaviour, but I was only talking to my friends. (Katherine)

Fumi complained about the state of the toilet. According to her the prison officer replied:

You are lucky to have one. . . . In your own country you would have to go to the bush.

Black women get put on report for 'kissing their teeth', which is considered rude by white officers. When black women are talking they tend to be loud and expressive and when they see a friend they tend to get excited and use their hands to express themselves. This is often misconstrued as aggressive behaviour and some women were put on report for it—in effect for behaving differently to whites.

Strip searches

Eighteen of the women talked about strip searches which every prisoner is subjected to on her first day in prison and also when she is transferred from one prison to another. They felt that there should be a private room for this purpose:

I did not like to be strip searched in front of the officers. It is very embarrassing and humiliating. (Miriam)

Ten of the women believed that black visitors were subjected to strip searches more than other people:

When it is a black woman they really do a thorough search. I did not have many visitors in prison . . . Who would want to come and be strip searched like that? (Jackie)

When it is a black visitor they really harass them and take their time in strip searching them. (Maureen)

114

Food and hygiene

All the women expressed concern about prison conditions. They said one prison was very dirty and talked about cockroaches, especially at the closed prison. One woman said:

> I was in a dormitory with eight women. We all used the same sink. It was pathetic. In prison you can catch anything. (Dawn)

Ten of the women complained about the food. They felt that better and healthier food should be provided, for themselves (and for their children). One woman said:

> I lost two stones whilst in prison. I could not eat the food. My face was so spotty. Nobody could recognise me on release. (Maxine)

Those women with children with them in prison complained about the food the children were getting:

> You have to buy decent food from your child benefit money. The food for the children is not good and there is no variety—children are not given fruits so mothers who get fruit with their meals keep it for their children. (Annette)

Medication

The women felt that that what women needed was counselling rather, for example, than psychotropic drugs. The higher rates of offences against prison discipline and the extensive prescription of tranquillisers and psychotropic drugs to female prisoners supports a claim that women's dependency aggravates their emotional and physical isolation.[27] As Bardsley recorded:

> One woman went in for importing cannabis. She came out addicted to Largactil.[28]

Visits

Several of the women talked about prisons being too far from their homes for relatives to travel. They said their families could not afford the fares, but they would have liked visits. For foreign women, isolation is compounded by not having visitors nor receiving money

---

[27] 'Sex and Sentencing', Morris A, *Criminal Law Review*, 1988, 163-171; Campell D, *The Guardian*, 11 January 1993.

[28] *Flowers in Hell*, Bardsley B, Pandora/Routledge, Kegan and Paul, 1987, p.75

from outside to buy essentials. Some of the foreign women lacked adequate clothing, as they were arrested at ports of entry with only one set of clothes and unsuitable shoes. Penny Green notes that:

> Women prisoners do not wear prison uniforms. They are therefore immediately disadvantaged if they have no friends or family to provide clothes for them. The vast majority of foreign nationals couriers arrive in Britain with an expectation of staying only five or so days—they bring enough clothes only for these few days, and if they arrive in summer they have no clothing adequate for the British winters ahead. Those they have with them are then all they have when they find themselves imprisoned for six to ten years. One Nigerian woman interviewed burst into tears and lifted her blouse to show she had no underwear at all, her plastic sandals were totally inadequate for the British climate. [29]

Children

A reason why some of the women from the United Kingdom were in an open prison was because they had their children with them, and therefore needed a mother and baby unit which does not exist in all women's prisons. Others were pre-occupied with worries relating to their children in the world outside, about how they were coping (this being exacerbated in the case of foreign women with children who were still abroad). They also worried about them not having enough money to live on. Some felt guilty about having friends or relatives looking after their children while they were in prison:

> You see the system is not fair. My friend who is herself unemployed is looking after my children and now the social security deduct money from her benefits because of my children. I feel bad about it. (Pam)

> The area I live is only whites there. I'm worried about my son because he is experiencing racism at school. (Alithea)

The women said that they preferred their own families to look after their children but realised the financial constraints when relatives were already 'struggling to make ends meet'. The women there were happy that they were able to go home for overnight leave every fortnight or once a month, as they could be with their children.

> I'm worried about my children. A friend is looking after them. I go home on leave every fortnight. They used to pay for your travelling expenses if you are doing a long sentence. They have stopped it since 1991. (Lorraine)

---

[29] See footnote 22.

116

(Foreign women find themselves in a situation where they might be unable to see their children for, say, five or more years—and may not be able to get in touch with relatives abroad to find out about them.) Often these women do not make child-care provisions in the hope or belief that they will be back within a week or so. They are told by drug barons that if caught they will be put on the next plane home. When they are sent to prison their children are left on their own with provisions for a week or so, or with relatives or friends who are told that the mother 'will be returning shortly'. The relatives or friends find it difficult to help the children financially for three or five years and the children have been known to die from lack of care and starvation.

FOREIGN NATIONALS DAY

I attended 'Foreign Nationals Day' in a closed women's prison as part of my research for this book. The women were to discuss the problems they were facing in prison and make suggestions. There were two groups—one conducted in Spanish and the one I attended which was conducted in English. It was attended by black women, mainly African-Caribbeans. The complaints of the women in this group centred around ill-treatment by prison officers and problems associated with making complaints, for example.:

- One woman felt that if you were outspoken and knew your rights you would find yourself in people's 'bad books' and that a transfer to an open prison would be refused as a form of 'punishment', which she was experiencing at the time.

- A black British woman talked about how she had found herself in trouble with prison officers by advising foreign black women of their rights. She said that whenever she felt the 'screws' were taking liberties with a foreign black woman she would explain to that woman her rights or speak to the 'screw' on her behalf. As a result, she had been labelled a 'big mouth' and a 'bad influence'. Despite having applied many times for a transfer to an open prison she still had not been granted this request.

- There was agreement from nearly all the women present that some prison officers treat them like children and not like human beings. The prison officer in the group said, 'If you treat us with respect we will treat you the same—otherwise you can't speak to us anyhow, if you ask nicely we'll listen'.

- Some women raised issues about the procedure for complaining to the governor about a prison officer. They said that if they wanted to make a complaint they had to go to a prison officer who would ask them the name of the prison officer they were complaining about, and he or she would then warn that officer. The women also said it was difficult, when asked who they were complaining about, to say 'It's you'. The women also felt that some of their complaints were not taken on board and that the prison governor did not get to hear about them.

- One of the women prison officers who was in the meeting stated that there was a way of complaining where it was necessary to write down the complaint so that no-one would know about it apart from the governor. The women disagreed with her. This was sound in theory but they knew very well that it was not possible to complain about a prison officer without the officers knowing about the subject of the complaint before the governor received it.

- One Rastafarian woman who had been doing pottery since she was in prison, talked about the need for black women to unite and work together. This was said to refer to some problems they had encountered in organizing the 'Foreign Nationals Day'. She said she was aware that many black women were experiencing problems in prison and that she was also aware how difficult it was to cope with these. She said that, as a Rastafarian woman, she was experiencing more problems than other women, as the whole prison culture was alien to her—'the food and everything is not what I'm used to'.

Mature advice

This last woman went on to advise black women in prison, especially the young ones, to use their prison time constructively and not to spend it dwelling on the negative side of imprisonment. She had a sample of some of the pottery she had made whilst in prison and displayed this. She said she had not done pottery before, but when she arrived in prison she felt that instead of spending her time dwelling on her problems and the 'unfair sentence' she got, she would attend classes and learn something.

She reminded the younger black women of the value of obtaining a certificate whilst in prison and how that certificate could help them to get a job on release. One young woman in the group was complaining about her experiences with prison officers and felt very aggrieved with the way she had been treated. She advised her to see time spent in prison as a time to rebuild her life, and not as wasted, and to join an education class and leave the prison with a certificate. She may have been seen by other women prisoners, especially the young ones, as something of a role model.

FUTURE INTENTIONS

During the interviews the women also talked about their intentions on release, thereby giving some insight into their attitudes to their offences and the effect that involvement with the criminal justice process had had on them. Many were preoccupied with worries about their employment prospects and accommodation, and what their communities would think of them as ex-prisoners. This is the subject matter of the final chapter.

Chapter 8

Hopes and Ambitions

This final chapter looks at the hazards faced by black women after a sentence has been completed. It examines their hopes, ambitions, attitudes and future plans. On their release black women still face all the problems of race, gender and class, but now exacerbated by the fact that they are now also ex-prisoners. The chapter concludes with a number of thoughts about the need for change put forward by the women and my own suggestions.

PROBLEMS ON RELEASE

For whatever reason, on release from prison fewer black people appear to seek and obtain help from the welfare services (including the probation service which is responsible for post-release supervision in those situations where this applies). The evidence is largely anecdotal, but it is hardly surprising because, as a general feature, black people resist any arrangements which they believe are part of a process which is discriminatory or 'not for them'. By way of example, one woman in the interview sample had not attended post-release group sessions because she found that the discussions did not relate to black people and that she in turn could not relate to the group. She said:

> It was all right for jobs and that, but you couldn't really discuss your problems as they would not be able to understand them.

There are other difficulties. In general, if someone is sent to prison this normally results in loss of employment and disruption of other ties to their community, family and associates. Other people 'move on' when someone is in prison so that a black woman, in particular, already at risk of being shunned by her former friends and possibly her family on whom she has 'brought disgrace' or unwanted attention from the authorities, may find it hard to re-establish former associations. The stigma of imprisonment is much stronger for black women than it is for people from other groups, so that they may receive little or no support on the one hand whilst coping with discrimination in relation to employment, accommodation and possible fresh involvement with the criminal justice process on the other.

Aisha Tarzi found the stigma of being in prison daunting for the women involved, in particular those from Asia, Africa and South America where a prison sentence is often seen as bringing dishonour and disgrace upon a family. As a result, family members may lose their jobs, engagements may be broken-off and wedding plans cancelled. Marriages can break up and children may be affected in various ways. In some of those countries the prisoners' family is ostracised and forfeits prestige.[1]

Anne Celnick noted that only 40 per cent of black offenders compared to 88 per cent of white offenders claimed that they were given help from family members.[2] Again, in her findings this is largely because of the disgrace brought upon the black person's family by the ex-prisoner. There may be 'guilt by association' for such family members (compare the comments on the policing of young men and the affect on their mothers contained in *Chapter 3*) and the black person's family or associates will not want to be thought of as suspects, or otherwise 'criminalised'. They may worry about finding *themselves* in trouble with the law just because they help a relative who has been to prison.

The same kind of considerations prevent some family members from visiting black relatives in prison, or from being supportive in other ways. Sixteen of the women interviewed expressed their concern about the stigma that attaches to having been in prison, and were worried about how their community might react to them if people found out where they had been (this often having been avoided so far). Only two of the women said they had supportive families.

MAKING PLANS

Universally, the women wanted a job when released from prison.[3] Their plans also included 'looking after the children' and 'getting on with life'.

---

[1] 'Victims of Freedom', Tarzi, A, in *Minority Ethnic Groups in the Criminal Justice System*, Gelsthorpe L (Ed), University of Cambridge Institute of Criminology, 1993.

[2] 'Race and Rehabilitation', Celnick A, in *Minority Ethnic Groups in the Criminal Justice System*, Gelsthorpe L (Ed.), University of Cambridge Institute of Criminology, 1993.

[3] Unemployment rates for all the main racial minorities are higher than for whites. Unemployment among white people in Britain is just under 10 per cent but soars to 24 per cent amongst Caribbeans and 38 per amongst Africans *(The Voice*, 15 February 1994).

Employment

Sixteen of the women were unemployed at the time of their arrest. Dawn, explaining why she was without a job said:

> I was unemployed because I do not want a low paid—and dirty—job. Why should I—it is very easy to get a low paid job—why should I take a low paid job with unsociable hours? I feel I have a lot to offer, if only they would give me the chance. The kind of job I want careerwise is what black people do not get—as black people we just get pushed to the back of the line.

Poverty among ethnic minority groups is directly connected to unemployment, low pay, industrial structures and racism. Many black women are unemployed or forced into jobs which attract low pay. Those black people who are employed are concentrated in those sectors with the lowest wages, such as distribution, hotels and catering, clothing and leather goods manufacture, and the lower rungs of the medical and health sectors.[4]

For Aisha, the whole 'system' was discriminatory:

> I think the system is like that—we are treated differently. It starts from the time you go to school; you get belittled you get labelled automatically. This is why half of the children end up not going to school—when you check it up—really we get treated in a particular way.

She went on to talk about equal opportunities policies:

> They go on with all this race harmony and equal rights—that's . . . just to quieten things down—to make things look good. As far as I am concerned when they say equal rights—equal education—that's just a cover up. When you get underneath you find something completely different . . . My friends found that each time they tick a box to say they are black British or black African they do not get an interview. We now know if you don't tick a box you stand a better chance of getting an interview. For example, if you fill in a housing form you get asked what ethnic group you belong to. I just leave that part blank—saying black British would not help—otherwise you get categorised automatically.

Generally speaking, the women were aware of the constraints imposed on them as black women, but at the same time they wanted to

---

[4] 'Poverty in Black and White: Deprivation and Ethnic Minorities, Amin and Oppenheim, Child Poverty Action Group with the Runnymede Trust, 1992.

change their poverty stricken lives. They would need a rehabilitation programme which would include helping them to get employment.

It seems important to note the historical and cultural background to the problems of black people in Britain[5] and how longstanding and deeply rooted are the difficulties—particularly as this affected the women's perceptions about the course their lives would take. Aisha, aged 23, talked about how her parents had suffered racism when they first came to this country and of her determination to overcome prejudice. She was not prepared to tolerate it as she was British:

> From the 1960s things have changed a bit. My parents came here as students and had a hard time . . . I'm British and am not standing for it . . . I know its going to be very hard to change the system − and its in the system − in some way I feel its going to be always like that . . . But I'm born here and feel I have more rights.

Dawn, who felt that she should be treated like everyone else as she was born here, said:

> As far as I'm concerned I'm British, I was born here − obviously white British do not think so − they often tell me to go back to where I come from − even the police have told me that − I tell them I was born here. . . and I *was* born here.

De Cook points out that black ex-prisoners are in a sense denied restoration to full citizenship because they have never received it in the first place. Full citizenship implies acceptance by other members of society.[6] More often than not, black people known to have been convicted of an offence continue to be stigmatised—even within their own communities—after they have completed their punishment. Failure to achieve full citizenship may itself be a barrier to reform. Black *people* are disadvantaged and black *offenders* doubly so.

Even nowadays it seems that being *born* in the United Kingdom does not necessarily convey full citizenship if you are black. Because of the colour of their skin, black people are viewed as illegal immigrants constantly having to prove that they are legitimately here, or born here:

> When I was coming from Jamaica, the customs officers found two ounces of cannabis on me. When they arrested me, they took my British passport

---

[5] See *Appendix I: Historical Background to Modern-Day Problems of 'Immigrant' Labour in Britain*

[6] 1993.

and I insisted on showing them my British birth certificate. They said 'Why are you showing us that?' When the duty solicitor came to see me he asked where I was born. I said I was British and that they had my passport. He said that when they called him they told him they had a Jamaican woman in custody. (Marion)

Accommodation

Black women are often caught in a vicious circle on release. When they are sent to prison their children may be placed with relatives or taken into local authority care. African-Caribbean women in Britain tend to live in council housing, usually flats. This means that if they are sent to prison they will lose their accommodation. Women who are sent to prison for longer than six months have to re-apply for housing, as they are viewed as having made themselves intentionally homeless (in effect, by committing a crime). It means that, on release, they have no accommodation to go to and therefore they cannot get their children back from the local authority which has taken them into care.

Several of the women in the sample were constantly worrying about this, especially those close to their release date. Eighteen had council accommodation and living under the threat that the council would take their property back if they were going to be in prison for longer than *six months*. The Housing Benefit, Council Tax Benefit and Income Support (Amendments) Regulations 1995 ended the practice of using housing benefit to meet the rent payments of convicted prisoners serving up to *a year* in custody. The change applied in respect of new single prisoners entering prison from April 1995 onwards.

The regulations also limited to a maximum of 13 weeks the time for which housing benefit can be paid in respect of an empty property from which a sentenced prisoner is temporarily absent. (The change did not affect unconvicted and unsentenced prisoners, who continue to be eligible for assistance for up to 52 weeks). Under the previous regulations, prisoners serving sentences of up to two years were eligible for assistance, because account was taken of the fact that those serving sentences of this length receive conditional or supervised release after half of their sentence, unless release is delayed as a punishment for a disciplinary offence. Under the present system, assistance is confined to prisoners serving sentences of up to six months, who are normally released unconditionally after 13 weeks in custody.

Other changes in the housing benefit regulations have increased homelessness among released prisoners.[7] The changes have increased

---

[7] 'Housing Benefit and Prisoners', Penal Affairs Consortium, 1996.

the likelihood that prisoners serving between 13 and 52 weeks will lose their homes and possessions. The report states:

> The removal of housing benefit from prisoners serving more than 13 weeks in custody has increased homelessness among released prisoners. We estimate that up to 5,000 additional prisoners could be released homeless each year as a result of this change, losing stable accommodation and all their furniture and possessions. This measure has had particularly harsh consequences for single mothers, often with devastating results for them and their young children.

Such children are often affected in the case of women prisoners because women are more likely than men to be sole carers. When children have been taken into care during a sentence, the loss of accommodation makes it less likely that they will be returned to their mother. When children have been looked after by relatives or friends and returned to their mother on release, if she has lost her home the family faces the prospect of starting again in 'bed and breakfast' and other unsatisfactory forms of accommodation. 'Homelessness and destitution on release greatly increase the risk of reoffending', says the report. It cites research showing that prisoners who are released homeless are more than twice as likely to reoffend as those with homes, and argues:

> Any money saved by the change is likely to be lost several times over by the costs of further offending, including the cost of police time, court time and further prison sentences. In short, this change is short-sighted, inhumane and counter-productive.

Under the new regulations, anyone serving over 13 weeks in prison cannot receive housing benefit at all. Local authorities have no discretion, for example, to pay for a few weeks to bridge any gap. Also, as some local authorities insist on four weeks' notice to terminate a tenancy, even if the prisoner acts promptly to give notice, four weeks' arrears accrue which the prisoner owes on release and must clear before being considered for rehousing as a homeless person.

The Penal Affairs Consortium has illustrated the impact of the changes by citing a series of cases in which prisoners have lost their homes and possessions as a result of the regulations.[8] The Consortium calls on the government to reinstate prisoners' eligibility for housing benefit to enable them to keep their homes during periods of up to 12

---

[8] 'Housing Benefit and Prisoners', Penal Affairs Consortium, 1996, pp 5-7.

months in custody. Commenting, Mary Honeyball, General Secretary of the Association of Chief Officers of Probation (ACOP), said:

> This change in eligibility has been one of the meanest yet made by the Department of Social Security. As a result of it, confusion and misinformation dominate housing benefit claims by prisoners, inadvertent arrears are disqualifying people from housing lists, and possessions that cannot be stored by prisoners evicted in their absence are having to be thrown away then on their release, when rehabilitation is crucial, they have no stable home to go to.
>
> There seems little logic in a policy that cuts benefits to create 'savings' when those same cuts actually cause greater expense in other departments. There is still less logic in making ex-prisoners homeless when we know it is such a powerful trigger in causing crime. It has been callous, costly and, by contributing to crime, entirely counter-productive as a useful public policy.

Paul Cavadino, chair of the Penal Affairs Consortium, concluded that:

> When courts pass prison sentences, they sentence offenders to be deprived of their liberty. They do not sentence them to lose their homes, their possessions and their children, yet that has been the effect of last year's housing benefit rules. This inhumane change should be reversed without delay.

One woman prisoner said:

> I am worried about losing my council flat. My outside probation officer is helpful. The council want the flat back and I have two children who are with my sister at the moment. (Judith)

Miriam who was in prison for handling stolen goods wanted a transfer from where she was living. She was constantly worrying about going back to the notorious council estate in north-west London which she felt was not a good place to bring up children:

> I am worrying too much about my children and about where I am going to live when I finish my prison sentence—I would like to leave the estate—or the area altogether. I need a transfer. I have been asking for a transfer for a long time but they still have not transferred me. I know if I go back to that estate I'll be back here again . . . things are so hard. There is a lot of crime on the estate—for example drugs—it is not good for the children—they come up selling some really nice clothes for the children and very cheap

127

price! You just find yourself tempted to buy as you want your children to look nice. I don't want that temptation again.

A TIME FOR REFLECTION

Several of the women spoke of the impact which imprisonment had had on them and, in some cases, how this would affect them in the future:

> No way would I find myself in such a situation again. I don't smoke or take drugs . . . I was forced to bring those drugs. I just want to do my sentence and leave. (Dorothy)

> This was my first time in trouble with the law . . . It is my first time in prison. I know what I did was wrong and risky, but at the time I was desperate for money to feed and clothe my children. (Jane)

Monica said that she had 'found God' whilst in prison and spoke of her future as follows:

> I regret that I did mix with the wrong crowd and got myself involved in handling stolen goods. I have now found God . . . and now believe in God . . . I will be living a clean, Christian life when I leave here.

She felt that if she had not been in prison she would not have seen the need to change her life:

> Prison has given me time to think about my life and to have time to study the Bible.

Doreen, who was on probation said:

> I have now decided to go to college. It is of my own accord. It's got nothing to do with me having been in prison or on probation. You have to make a decision at some time in your life.

THE CRIMINAL JUSTICE PROCESS

Whatever the theory may be about Britain being a multi-racial society it is clear from the earlier chapters of this book this ideal is far from a reality. Throughout those chapters, the women in the sample are quoted putting forward ideas, suggestions and criticisms of the criminal justice process. The following random items serve to give some indication of the women's perceptions and thus the scale of the problem which needs to be overcome if black women are to accept that criminal justice can be delivered in what they see as a largely male dominated, white, Euro-centric society:

There should be a change in police custody. The way they talk to you like you are not a human being—they have to change the way they handle people. They abuse their power and some are racist. (Karen)

One day I was at the social security and there was some trouble there and they (police officers) came to arrest a man—a whole lot of them, including a police sergeant in the lift. I pressed a lift to go downstairs and the sergeant said to me 'look at your black cunt'. That's what he said to me—the sergeant—and they were all laughing. So I abused him back. You have to know your rights in this country otherwise they will walk all over you. (Alithea)

There was no black jury in my case. I feel black people would understand you better. (Rhona)

There should be more black lawyers, probation officers and police officers. This would give us more confidence in dealing with them. Even though my black probation officer was not helpful, I still feel more comfortable talking to black professionals. (Sarah)

More black judges would make a difference—whites need to see us as human beings. (Lorraine)

There should be more black prison officers otherwise its like 'them against us'—you see. (Dawn)

Some black lawyers give you the impression 'I have gone that one step further and I'm better than you.' I still feel we need more black lawyers though. (Aisha)

I live on a very notorious council estate in London. They went and employed five black officers and they were given hell—as sell outs. When they are doing their raids they try to include a black officer. It may help if they employed a black officer from the black community—from the ghetto not those who were brought up in a white area. Older black people there got listened to better than the police. (Marva)

129

There should be more black lawyers because I feel that some white solicitors are still racist — they press you to plead guilty because they are convinced that you did commit the crime. (Rhona)

I don't think having more black lawyers would make a difference — it would come to the same thing — there are some black lawyers who think, or are, more white than whites. (Judith)

The solution is not to have more black police officers or lawyers but to accept black people as they are. Black people have to sacrifice their identity to get on in life. You can't work for the system — remaining black — and getting promoted. When black people are too professional they become white minded — they put on airs and graces — that is the only way they can be accepted and succeed in this system. (Aisha)

SOME CONCLUDING THOUGHTS

The experiences of the women described in this book support the view that although there are many problems which women as a whole share, there are added problems for black women and that the colour of their skin has a bearing on the way they are dealt with by the criminal justice process. Whatever the laudable and extensive initiatives taken by government departments and criminal justice agencies to combat racialism and discrimination, the situation can be described as one in which the substance of what is actually happening does not match the grand structures which are being built around issues of discrimination. How else can it be explained in the wake of section 95 Criminal Justice Act 1991, the publication of extensive data and other information by the Home Office and the development of a range of activities to combat discrimination by individual criminal justice agencies that the number of black people and women being drawn into the criminal justice process and ultimately into the prisons is still disproportionate and rising?

Making things happen
There is every difference between acknowledging the existence of a problem, saying that mechanisms have been put in place, and actually changing outcomes. Thus far, a grand agenda has failed to deliver overall improvement in the way that ethnic minorities, women and black women in particular are dealt with. Indeed, there has been a deterioration in terms of equal outcomes. Perhaps the one saving feature is that section 95 itself is still in place when in other parts of Europe and around the world such 'protections' have tended to

recede. A change of government in 1997 might be seen by the new administration as an opportunity to turn the sentiments behind statutory provision into positive action. It is a question of making *things happen* not just hoping or believing that they will. With this in mind, there are a number of suggestions which I can advance based on the issues raised in this book and with particular emphasis on the situation of black women as one of those 'discreet' and 'identifiable' minority groups referred to in *Chapter 1* and which believe that justice is for other people and 'not for them':

- there should be ready acceptance by people in senior positions within the criminal justice process that racism and discrimination on the grounds of race or gender still exists and that there is a need to re-double existing efforts if the behaviour of the very many decision-makers for whom they are responsible or accountable is to change.

- the training and information that is available should concentrate on making decision-makers more aware of the perceptions and cultures of minority groups with a view to avoiding stereotyping and misleading assumptions about black people, about women and about black women (*Chapters 1* and 2).

- there should be recognition of the multiple disadvantages faced by black women and of their general sense that they do not receive justice (*Chapters 1* and 8).

- there should be better understanding of black women's lives and a recognition that in a multi-cultural society these may not accord with the middle-class values of white women (whether feminists, criminologists or ordinary people) from the dominant culture —indeed there is no reason why they should. Diversity should not be made to read 'criminal propensity' (see, generally *Chapter 2*).

- the police should display greater sensitivity to the kind of matters concerning the interviewing, arrest and prosecution of black women and should recognise that failure to do so may be counter-productive in that many black women are likely to be alienated. In particular, the police should recognise that the action they take has a significant effect on responses at later stages in the criminal justice process. Black women should not be

131

treated as if they were 'illegal immigrants' and 'guilt by association' or 'secondary punishment' should be avoided (*Chapter 3*).

- caution should attach to the use of mental health powers if action relies on black women not behaving 'normally'(something that applies at all stages of the criminal justice process, but see, particularly *Chapter 3*).

- the probation service should continue its progressive work but with greater emphasis being placed on the special problems of black women in terms of the provision of information to courts, community sentences and other facilities and resources which are *relevant* to black women. It should not be assumed that the existence of strong equal opportunity and anti-discrimination policies and practices will automatically guarantee equality of opportunity and the absence of discrimination (*Chapter 4*).

- sustained efforts should be made to recruit black people, including black women into the higher ranks of the judiciary and black lawyers who might progress to such posts should not be denigrated or discouraged in their day-to-day dealings in court (*Chapter 5*).

- all people concerned with the administration of the courts and with judicial decision-making should obtain a clearer understanding of issues affecting black people and should consider that data which shows how black people and women have been dealt with up until now. The duty to deal fairly and impartially with *all* people should not be allowed to mask the fact that, on the evidence, that duty has not been fully discharged, something which does not seem to have improved in recent years despite extensive training and the availability of improved information in this regard (*Chapter 5*).

- more appropriate and relevant provision should be made for the increasing number of black women (including black foreign women) arriving in prison. There should be major efforts to combat racism and inequalities in prison discipline, as well as to build on the positive aspect that many black women wish to improve their education and future prospects before re-entering their communities. The use of medication, strip searches and psychiatric provision should be carefully monitored to ensure that these do not involve a racist or discriminatory element (*Chapter 7*).

- the fact that black women are faced with multiple hazards of discrimination should be a feature recognised and understood by people across the criminal justice process and, once brought to attention, should feature prominently on the agenda of all people concerned with equality of treatment.

APPENDIX I: HISTORICAL BACKGROUND TO MODERN-DAY PROBLEMS OF 'IMMIGRANT' LABOUR IN BRITAIN

The first generation to come to Britain in the 1950s and 1960s was actually *invited*. The flow of immigrant labour into post-war Britain was not some 'hostile invasion'. The old British Empire offered the United Kingdom a solution to the problem of acute labour shortages. Thus, for instance, London Transport recruited bus crews in the West Indies and, as Minister of Health (1960-63), Enoch Powell actively encouraged the recruitment of West Indian and Asian nurses by British hospitals. Indeed, for some people, the prospect of losing this cheap source of immigrant labour was worrying:

> In the hot and heavy industry such as foundries – never popular in times of full employment with the home labour force – they [immigrants] frequently constitute the only available pool of labour. In the textile industry, it has been claimed that night shifts would be forced to close down entirely without them. (*The Times*, 4 August 1965)

Although essentially racist, such sentiments acknowledge the significant part immigrant labour played in the burgeoning economy of the early 1960s, but at the same time, show the historically vulnerable position of black labour in British society. When an economic boom is followed by a recession, unskilled labourers are often the hardest hit, as the poverty experienced by black people in Britain in the 1990s also shows. Many of the jobs which the first generation had were the dirtiest, often the most hazardous, involving shift work and were frequently in the worst-paid manual occupations. Previous experience and skills were ignored by employers and black workers were increasingly placed in 'new' jobs on the shop floor, opened up by changes in technology—for example, in the iron foundry industry in the West Midlands—where they were shunned by unions and white workers alike, who were concentrated in the older, established artisan and skilled jobs.

The conditions and levels of pay were compounded by racism and discrimination, which were experienced daily, ranging from routine protests by white workers against employing black people to notices saying 'No coloureds' at factory gates.[1]

Also, the first generation experienced housing problems. Widescale research disclosed that black people were living in squalid

---

[1] 'Ethnic Minorities and Employment', Block 4, Open University Press, 1982.

and overcrowded conditions, mainly in the private rented sector.[2] Often this was in 'lodging houses' in inner cities, along with friends and relatives, but this accommodation was not cheap. Landlords often charged a premium, branded a 'newcomers' tax', or 'foreigner levy'. Before legislation made blatant racism unlawful, landlords discriminated openly against black people by displaying signs bearing slogans like: 'No coloureds. No Irish. No dogs.' The housing levels of black people have not changed significantly. Many immigrants and black people who are British-born live in poor housing conditions in inner cities, and still undertake unskilled or semi-skilled employment.

The older generation remains God fearing and law-abiding, their offspring, often British born, has become criminalised. The second generation is seen to be 'rising up', or 'angry', in refusing low level employment or shiftwork (where there is any to refuse) and generally struggling, or 'hustling', to survive in a variety of ways—legal, semi-legal and illegal.[3]

---

[2] Newham Monitoring Project.

[3] 'The Racism of Criminalisation: Police and the Production of the Crimnal Other in Minority Ethnic Groups', Jefferson T, 1993.

Index

A

ABPO 50
accommodation 125
ACPO 29
ACOP 50 127
Adler, F 22
African-Caribbeans
    definition 11
aggression, black female 22 33 35
    52 54 56
Alexander v. Home Office 1988 107
Alien Deportation Group 34
Ali, Mohammed 41
Anglicised 54
applications (prison) 106
'arm-waving' 33
arrest 30 32 *et al*
Asians 33 67
assumptions about black
    people/black women 30 49 53
    63 65 74 107 131

B

bail 30 70 73 74 79
Bail Act 1976 74
Bar/barristers 15 75
Bardsley, B 115
Beatrice's case 19 87
Bernard, C 27
black, meaning in this book 11
Black People in Magistrates' Courts
    15 64
black women prison scheme 33
Brixton riots 39
Broadwater Farm 36 39
Browne, D 43
'brownness' 24

C

Campaign Against Racism and
    Fascism 41
Campaign for Racial Equality
    (CRE) 29 31
Canaan, A 24
'canteen culture' (police) 29
cautioning 29 32
Cautions v. Prosecutions 29
Celnick, A 122
children (worries about) 116
chivalry 25 36
citizenship, full 124
class 14
coconuts 59
codes of practice 15
community sentences 51
court decision-making 66
court personnel 63
Court Service 63
courts 66 *et al*
Criminal Justice Act 1991 11 49
    51 (see also section 29)
criminal justice process 11
Criminal Justice Consultative
    Council 15
Criminal Justice and Public Order
    Act 1994 49
criminology 21 *et al*
Crowe and Cove 71
Crown Court 63 67 *et al* 77
Crown Prosecution Service (CPS)
    15 30 70 75 78
'Cynic', 'Sergeant' 41

D

DeCook 124
demeanour 66
Denning, Lord 65
Denny, D 54
depressed/depression 55

disadvantage 11 28 53
discontinuance 30
discount for/effect of plea 30 58 67
discipline (prison) 106 112
discrimination 15 28 49 65 105 123
disgrace 121
distance 103
Dobash, Dobash and Gutteridge 113
domestic violence 34
dominant values 11 53 65
drugs/drug use 27 28 88 128
drug smuggling 15
Dunn, J 44
duty solicitors 76 81

E

education 13 14 109
Elton, Lord 11
employment 123
ethnic minorities 30
Ethnic Minorities Advisory Committee (JSB) 63
Ethnic Origin of Prisoners 68
Euro-centric view of society 53 129

F

Fahy, T 44
family/families 25 51 52 54 72 104 116 121 122
fathers 14
feeble-mindedness 21
feminist criminology 21 *et al*
Fitzgerald, M 69
food 115
Foreign Nationals Day 117
foreign women 13 15 104
Fry 25

G

gatekeeping 51
Gardner, Joy 34
Gelsthorpe, L 21 52
gender 12 13 21 25 26
Genders and Player 106
Gordon, P 40
Gorman, Teresa 35
Graef, Roger 31
Greater London Council (GLC) 31
guilt by association (secondary punishment) 14

H

harassment 32 105
Hedderman, C 66
Heidensohn, F 22
helpline 64
homelessness 126
Home Office 63 105 108
    Statistical Bulletin 21/94 68
Home Secretary, duty 15
Honeyball, M 127
Hood, Roger 66
Hooks, B 25
housing benefit 125
Hudson, B 55
hygiene 115
hysterical 33

I

'illegal immigrants' 33 40
immigrants 33 40 135
initiatives 29 49 63 101
Inspector of Prisons 113
interviews 46 56 77 108
    method 16

J

jobs (prison) 107 109

judges 63 64 67
Judicial Studies Board (JSB) 15 63

K

Kennedy, Helena 26 27 34 65 76
King, J 52
'kissing teeth' 114

L

labelling 52
language problems 104
Law Society 15
lawyers 75 81
Lord Chancellor/Lord
    Chancellor's Department 15 63
    64
Leonard, E 23
Lewis, D 25
Lipsidge, M 44
Littlewood, R 44

M

magistrates 63 64 77
male
    'Chronicle of Male Action' 23
matriarch, black 13
mature advice 117-118
media reports 35
medical reports 50
medication 44 115
mental deficiency/disorder 21 33
    42 *et al* 103
Merseyside Probation Service 54
MIND 43 45 46
mode of trial 30
Morris, A 22
myths, about black people/black
    women 53
    (see also assumptions)

N

NACRO 15 63 73
NAPO 50 53 73 102
National Standards 49 58
Newcastle, muggings 32
Newham Monitoring Project 36
'nig nogs' 78
not guilty pleas 30 58 67

O

opportunities to commit crime 23
Osler, A 52

P

Padel and Stevenson 106
parents, single 26 33
Penal Affairs Consortium 12 13
    33 51 72 126 127
personality disorder 103
petitions 106
Pickles, Judge 78
Pinder, R 75
plans 122
Player, E 47
police 29 *et al*
    culture 29 31
Police Complaints Authority 38
Police Monitoring and Research
    Group 45
Policing and Racial Equality 29
poverty 14 28
power, lack of 24 54
prayer letter, 98
prejudice 32
pre-sentence reports (PSRs) 49 *et
    al*
prestige, forfeited 122
previous convictions 68
prison/Prison Service 101 *et al*
prison officers 110
probation 49 *et al*
prostitution 32
psychotropic drugs 115

139

psychoses 103
punishment 56

Q

quality control of PSRs 61

R

race 12
Race and the Criminal Justice System
 15
race and criminal justice 69
racism 29 32 48 63 105 113
Race Relations Manual (prison) 102
 105
Rastafarian 105
Reiner, R 40
release 121
remand 70
Resource Pack (Merseyside
 Probation Service) 54
Roberts, C 23
Royal Commission on Criminal
 Procedure 29 69
Rumbold, Angela 105
Runnymead Trust 74

S

'Sambo-Samaritan' 106
schizophrenia 44
secondary punishment 14
section 95 15 29 63 69 130
self-harm 103
sentence 80 104
*Sentencing Practice in the Crown
 Court* 51
shorter sentences for women 104
Simon, R 23
special difficulties for black
 women 104
Spellman, E 25
stereotyping 13 14 21 27 34 49
 54 56 105 107

stop and search 30 *et al*
strip searches 114

T

Tarzi, A 122
thematic reports, HM Inspector of
 Constabulary 29
traditional approaches to
 criminology 21
tranquillisers 115

U

unemployment 72

V

Victorian England 21
visits 115
Voakes and Fowler 74
Voice, The 32 78

W

Waters, R 55
welfare, shift away from in
 probation 51
West Midlands 67
What's Next in the Law? 65
Whitehouse, P 53 54
Wolverhampton study 68
women
 Asian 33
 bail 73
 capable of crime 14
 courts, and 71
 imprisonment 102
 interview sample 16
 probation etc 52
 prisoners 108

Z

Zedner, L 21

Some other Waterside Press Titles

CRIMINAL JUSTICE, CRIMINAL POLICY AND SENTENCING

Introduction to the Criminal Justice Process Bryan Gibson and Paul Cavadino. 'Rarely, if ever, has this complex process been described with such comprehensiveness and clarity': *Justice of the Peace*. (First reprint, 1997) ISBN 1 872 870 09 0. £12.00 plus £1.50 p&p

Introduction to the Magistrates' Court Bryan Gibson (Second edition) A clear outline and a *Glossary of Words, Phrases and Abbreviations* (750 entries). ISBN 1 872 870 15 5. £10.00 plus £1.50 p&p

Introduction to the Probation Service Anthony Osler. An overview, including a brief history and modern-day responsibilities ISBN 1 872 870 19 8. £10.00 plus £1.50 p&p

Transforming Criminal Policy Andrew Rutherford. Looks at 'Spheres of Influence' in the USA, The Netherlands and England and Wales in the 1980s. ISBN 1 872 870 31 7. £16.00 plus £1.50 p&p **Criminal Policy Series**

The Sentence of the Court: A Handbook for Magistrates Michael Watkins, Winston Gordon and Anthony Jeffries. Consultant Dr. David Thomas. Foreword by Lord Taylor, Lord Chief Justice. (Fourth reprint, 1996). ISBN 1 872 870 25 2. In use for magistrates' training in many parts of England and Wales. 'Excellent': *The Law*. £10.00 plus £1.50 p&p

A to Z of Criminal Justice Paul Cavadino (1997) ISBN 1 872 870 10 4. £18.00 plus £1.50 p&p

Criminal Justice and the Pursuit of Decency Andrew Rutherford. 'By reminding us that, without "good men and women" committed to humanising penal practice, criminal justice can so easily sink into apathy and pointless repression, Andrew Rutherford has sounded both a warning and a note of optimism.': *Sunday Telegraph* ISBN 1 872 870 21 X. £12.00 plus £1.50 p&p

Handbook of Effective Community Programmes Edited by Carol Martin. Published in association with the Institute for the Study and Treatment of Delinquency (ISTD). ISBN 1 872 870 44 9. £10.00 plus £1.50 p&p

YOUNG PEOPLE AND CRIME

Introduction to the Youth Court (incorporating *The Sentence of the Youth Court*). Winston Gordon, Michael Watkins and Philip Cuddy. Foreword by Lord Woolf, Master of the Rolls. Produced under the auspices of the Justices' Clerks' Society.

. . . a comprehensive, up-to-date and readable overview of its subject . . . Although there are a number of more substantial legal texts on youth court proceedings, this is the first that I feel places those proceedings sufficiently in context: Barry Anderson in the *Law Society Gazette*

. . . an extremely useful and up-to-date book of very handy size and reasonably priced for the information it contains . . . It is a must for those interested in the work of the youth courts: Brian Worster-Davis *The Magistrate*

ISBN 1 872 870 36 8. £12.00 plus £1.50 p&p

Children Who Kill Edited by Paul Cavadino. From the tragic Mary Bell and Jamie Bulger cases to events world-wide. Contributors include Gitta Sereny, Peter Badge, Dr. Norman Tutt and Dr. Susan Bailey. Published in conjunction with the British Juvenile and Family Courts Society (BJFCS). 'Highly recommended': *The Law* ISBN 1 872 870 29 5. £16.00 plus £1.50 p&p

Growing Out of Crime The New Era Andrew Rutherford. The classic and challenging work about young offenders. ISBN 1 872 870 06 6. £12.50 plus £1.50 p&p

Juvenile Delinquents and Young People in Trouble in an Open Environment Edited by William McCarney. An international survey of youth justice. Published in conjunction with the International Association of Juvenile and Family Court Magistrates (IAJFCM). ISBN 1 872 870 39 2. £18.00 plus £1.50 p&p

Introduction to the Scottish Children's Panel Alistair Kelly. The first basic book in 20 years on this topic. ISBN 1 872 870 38 4. £12.00 plus £1.50 p&p

SPECIAL INTEREST

Interpreters and the Legal Process Joan Colin and Ruth Morris. For all people who are interested in spoken language or sign language in the legal context. ISBN 1 872 870 28 7. £12.00 plus £1.50 p&p

Justice for Victims and Offenders Martin Wright (Second edition). A completely new and fully updated treatment of this highly regarded work. ISBN 1 872 870 35 X. £16.00 plus £1.50 p&p

Capital Punishment: Global Issues and Prospects Edited by Peter Hodgkinson and Andrew Rutherford. Deals with the topic world-wide. ISBN 1 872 870 32 5. £32.00 plus £1.50 p&p **Criminal Policy Series** 'This book will replace many other sources of information': *Justice of the Peace*

Relational Justice: Repairing the Breach Edited by Jonathan Burnside and Nicola Baker. Foreword by Lord Woolf. As featured in *The Guardian*. (1994) ISBN 1 872 870 22 8. £10.00 plus £1.50 p&p

Punishments of Former Days Ernest Pettifer (1992) 'A good read.': *The Magistrate* ISBN 1 872 870 05 8. £9.50 plus £1.50 p&p

FAMILY PROCEEDINGS

Introduction to the Family Proceedings Court Elaine Laken, Chris Bazell and Winston Gordon. Published under the auspices of the Justices' Clerks' Society. With a Foreword by Sir Stephen Brown, President of the Faimily Division of the High Court. (1997) ISBN 1 872 870 46 5. £12.00 + £1.50 p&p

An overview of the magistrates' family proceedings court, including a special section on domestic violence.

Criminal Classes: Offenders at School
Angela Devlin

ISBN 1 872 870 30 9. £16.00 plus £1.50 p&p

What the critics said:

'A wise and absorbing volume: if you are in any doubt about the links between poor education, crime and recidivism, read it': Marcel Berlins *The Guardian*

'An extremely frank and interesting insight': Victoria Myerson *The Law*

'Somebody buy this book for John Major': Peter Kingston *The Guardian*

'A book of considerable public importance which calls for attention': Sir Stephen Tumim

ALSO BY ANGELA DEVLIN

Prison Patter

A unique 'dictionary' of prison slang. ISBN 1 872 870 41 4. £12.00 plus £1.50 p&p

All the above books are available from Waterside Press, Domum Road, Winchester SO23 9NN Tel or fax 01962 855567. Cheques should be made payable to 'Waterside Press'. Please remember to add p&p